With Malice Toward All

With MALICE toward ALL

DOROTHY HERRMANN

G. P. PUTNAM'S SONS
NEW YORK

Published simultaneously in Canada by Academic Press
Canada Limited, Toronto.

Some material in this book appeared originally in *Cosmopolitan* in radically different form.

Library of Congress Cataloging in Publication Data

Herrmann, Dorothy.
With malice toward all.

Bibliography: p.
1. American wit and humor—History and criticism.
2. Humorists—United States—Biography. I. Title.
PS438.H4 1982 817'.52'09 81-15819
ISBN 0-399-12710-0 AACR2

PRINTED IN THE UNITED STATES OF AMERICA

Acknowledgments

I wish to thank Dorothy L. Swerdlove, Curator of the Theater Collection at the Library of the Performing Arts, Lincoln Center, New York, and her entire staff for their endless help to me in my research.

I am also indebted to Wendy Warnken, Associate Curator of the Theater Collection, Museum of the City of New York, and the staffs of the Mercantile Library Association of New York, the New York Public Library, the Columbia University Library, the Museum of Broadcasting, New York, and the Library of Congress, Washington, D.C.

I owe special thanks to Irving Kolodin, William S. Targ and Milton Goldman for giving me additional anecdotal material as well as their personal reminiscences of Oscar Levant, Tallulah Bankhead and Dorothy Parker.

Also my thanks to: Helen Gurley Brown, Owen Edwards, Guy Flatley, Ellen Goldberg, David Grambs, Dr. Philip Herzbrun, Charles Jules, Bill Krasnoborski, Dr. Jay Silverman, Jim Watters and Larry Whitney.

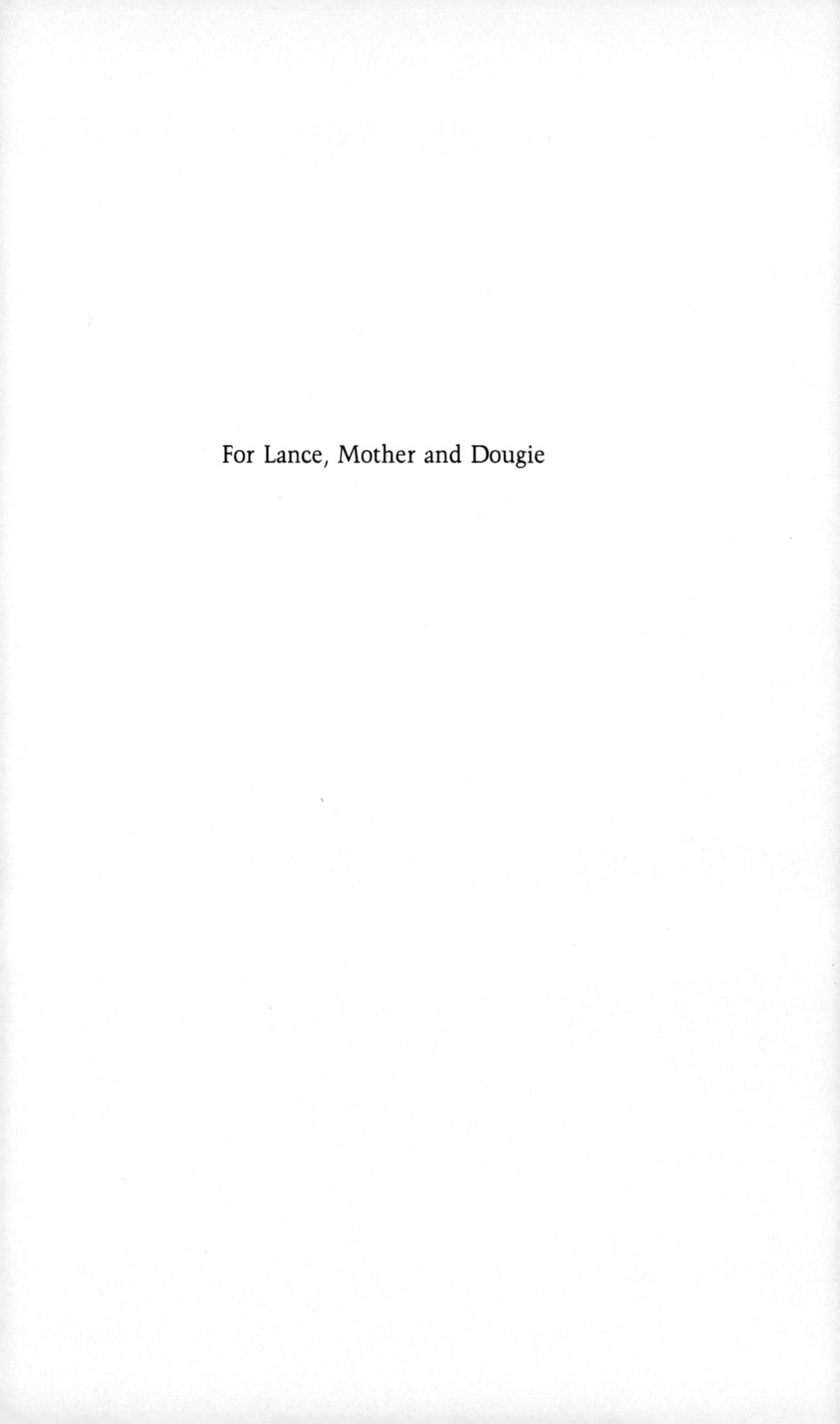

For Lance, Mother and Dougie

Contents

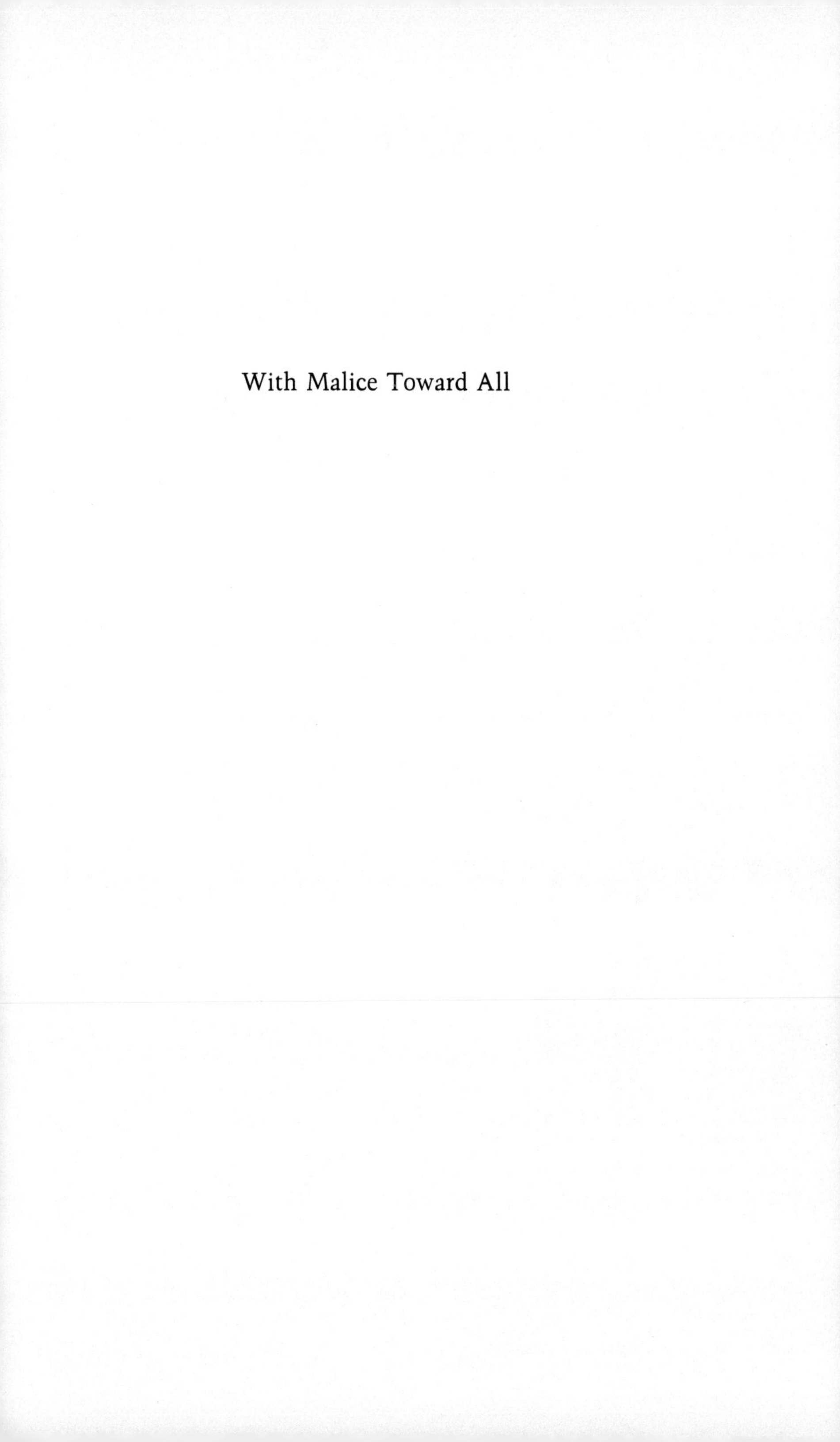

With Malice Toward All

Foreword

"*IMPROPRIETY IS* the soul of wit," said Somerset Maugham. The people in this book were certainly witty and in many cases improper. Their lives were struggles against conformity and their tongues were usually busy poking fun at stuffiness.

They were wisecrackers, verbal improvisers, masters of the bon mot and the cynical retort. Some were professionals who made a living out of being funny, but others were amateurs who used a drawing room or a restaurant as their stage. Some were rich, born in luxury, and some struggled out of tenements and shanties. Some were ugly, some beautiful, some were men, some women. But all had the rare gift of putting words together in fresh and arresting combinations that in their day made people laugh. All had the ability to think on their feet—and the cheek to say exactly what they pleased.

They were born jesters who added sparkle to many an occasion.

The people in this book flourished in the 1920s, 30s, and early 40s. All shared a time when America seemed less jaded and more innocent than today. It was a time before television, a time when conversational ability and wit were greatly valued. Fashionable people of the 20s might cultivate not one wit but several who would spur each other on to dazzling feats of wordplay. In speakeasies and restaurants like Reuben's and Lindy's, wisecracking was an art, a form of verbal jousting that commanded a large audience. At Lindy's, even the waiters were expected to wisecrack.

The best-known quipsters of this era were the wits of the Algonquin Round Table, who, being newspaper and magazine people, readily publicized themselves and each other. Alexander Woollcott, Dorothy Parker, Robert Benchley and George S. Kaufman were top performers in this group. But equally celebrated were Texas Guinan, the nightclub hostess who hurled breezy insults and homely comments at her patrons; W. C. Fields, who loved to make fun of women, children and his own drinking habits; Wilson Mizner, the brilliant, ne'er-do-well son of a prominent California family, called by some the wittiest man of his time; his brother Addison, a distinguished architect who launched the Spanish style in Florida; and Tallulah Bankhead, the beautiful Alabama madcap who tossed off many amusing one-liners in the course of her ceaseless chatter. There was also the pianist Oscar Levant, with his weary and cynical comments, and Groucho Marx, who was as outrageous offstage as on. And there was President Teddy Roosevelt's daughter, Alice Roosevelt Longworth ("Princess Alice"), who enjoyed terrorizing Washington society for almost a century.

Since so much of their art was conversational and passed along by word of mouth, the true authorship of some of their wisecracks has occasionally been hard to ascertain. I have consulted magazine profiles, newspaper articles of the period, and old family scrapbooks in an effort to pin down the truth. When the real author of a line has been impossible to determine, I have abided by Oscar Levant's principle: "It doesn't matter who says it first, it's who gets credit for it last that counts."

The lives of the people in this book were exciting and colorful, and many had talents aside from wisecracking. Woollcott, for instance, was a noted drama critic. Levant was a serious concert pianist and a composer of more than forty popular songs, including "Lady Play Your Mandolin." Tallulah Bankhead was a well-known actress on the stage and in motion pictures. Robert Benchley, Dorothy Parker and George S. Kaufman were all professional writers who produced plays, short stories, essays and poetry. Wilson Mizner was a jack-of-all-trades who did everything from selling patent medicines to managing Stanley Ketchel, the middleweight champion of the world. W. C. Fields and Groucho Marx were highly successful comedians and movie actors.

Their respective achievements, however, made few of them happy. Kaufman denigrated his talents as a playwright and contemptuously called himself "a play doctor." Benchley was ashamed of his work as a humorist and longed all his life to write a history of the Queen Anne era. Levant yearned to be as good a composer as his idol George Gershwin, and Groucho Marx said that his greatest ambition was to be a writer of stature. At the end of her life Dorothy Parker denounced her fame as a wit and a poet and excoriated herself bitterly for not having helped humanity.

It has often been said that comedy must go hand in hand with tragedy and that it springs from a miserable childhood. In this there may be some truth. Among the twelve talented men and women discussed in this book, five lost a mother or a brother in early life. Others had sickly or lonely childhoods, and in the case of W. C. Fields, one steeped in poverty and brutality. In later years, brilliant though their careers were, all had marital problems. Almost all of them suffered from insomnia, a symptom of inner conflict and anxiety. As they grew older, many of them depended more and more on alcohol and drugs, and some of them turned into full-fledged drunkards and addicts.

Nevertheless, none of the twelve were objects of pity. For in their heyday, they experienced the thrill of having a ceaseless audience for their verbal sallies. In the restaurants and drawing rooms they frequented, they were usually the life of the party. None of these wisecrackers was a true social critic, but in their most inspired bons mots a small explosive charge may often be found, guaranteed to unsettle the hypocritical and the pretentious. Best of all, their virtuosity was original. It needed no stable of gagwriters, no canned studio laughter. It sprang from their own lively brains, their brilliant impudent tongues, and that mysterious precious ingredient known as wit.

1

Alexander Woollcott

Knight of the Round Table

"All the things I like to do are either illegal, immoral or fattening."

ALTHOUGH NOBODY knows the exact date the Algonquin Round Table began, it was sometime around 1919. Its instigator was a man named John Peter Toohey. He was a theatrical press agent who was miffed because Alexander Woollcott, drama critic of *The New York Times*, had refused to put a plug in his column for Toohey's client, a struggling young playwright named Eugene O'Neill. To get back at Woollcott, Toohey decided to give a luncheon for him at the Algonquin Hotel, ostensibly to welcome him back from World War I. Woollcott was inordinately proud of the part he had played in the conflict as frontline correspondent for the Army newspaper, *The Stars and Stripes*. Toohey planned to invite other drama critics and newspaper people to the luncheon, among them Dorothy Parker, Robert Benchley and Franklin P. Adams.

The party was held in the Algonquin's Pergola Room,

which had a Bay of Naples mural along one wall and mirrors along the other. When Woollcott came in, the first thing he saw was a huge banner bearing the legend:

AWOL
cot
S. J. Kaufman, Post No. 1

The guest of honor paused and began to laugh. The banner not only demeaned Woollcott's army service, but it also embodied two of his greatest anathemas—the misspelling of his name and his hatred of S. J. Kaufman, a columnist for the *Telegram*, whom Woollcott regarded as a phony and a bad writer.

Toohey and his fellow pranksters then handed programs around. In each, twelve after-luncheon speeches were listed, all to be given by none other than Woollcott himself. Every time his name appeared, it was misspelled in a different way. All the speeches would deal with World War I and Woollcott's role in it.

The party was a huge success, and Woollcott had a wonderful time. Although it failed to deflate him, it began a tradition. As a press agent, Toohey was supposed to cultivate influential members of the press; somewhat self-servingly, he suggested that everyone present meet for lunch at the hotel every day. Carried away by the conviviality of the occasion, most of the guests thought it an excellent idea, and so began the Algonquin Round Table. It would last for over a decade.

The Algonquin Hotel on Manhattan's West 44th Street was already well known to New Yorkers in 1919. It boasted a devoted clientele of theatrical and literary people who were charmed not only by its quiet oak-paneled lobby, its fine Oriental rugs and massive carved grandfather clock, but by the fact that many successful artists and writers had lived and created there. Booth Tarkington and Richard Harding Davis had both written works in Algonquin rooms, and Paul Armstrong, a playwright of the 20s, had dashed off the hit comedy *Alias Jimmy Valentine* at the hotel in the space of only nine days.

Even before the inception of the Round Table, Robert Benchley, the humorist, and Heywood Broun, the journalist, had lunched frequently in the Algonquin dining room. So had actress Ethel Barrymore and her brother John as well as their uncle John Drew. Laurette Taylor, Ina Claire, Irvin S. Cobb and Commander Evangeline Booth of the Salvation Army were also among its devotees. Young Tallulah Bankhead, fresh from Alabama, had rented a room with bath there in 1918 for twenty-one dollars a week. Douglas Fairbanks, Sr., the great silent picture star, brought his family there on visits to New York, and kept in shape, according to legend, for his taxing motion-picture stunts by skipping rope each afternoon on the Algonquin roof.

The Algonquin was originally designed as an apartment house, but since few people rented its apartments, the owner converted the building into a hotel. He told his manager, Frank Case, that he was thinking of calling it "The Puritan." Case—a man of taste and intelligence—disagreed. That was too sanctimonious a name, he said, for a smart hotel in the heart of Manhattan. Hoping to come up with something livelier, he went down the street to the New York Public Library, where he learned that the first inhabitants of the neighborhood had been the Algonquin Indians. So the Algonquin it became and has been to this day.

When the Algonquin wits first started meeting at the hotel, they had no official name for their group nor did they sit at a round table. At lunch, which was scheduled for one o'clock sharp, they sat at a long rectangular table in the Pergola Room (now known as the Oak Room). But as the group grew, Frank Case moved it to a large round table in the center of the Rose Room. He also assigned the members their own waiter, one Luigi. By then the group had begun to call themselves "the Board" and their luncheons "the Board Meetings." They dropped these names in favor of "Luigi Board," then supplanted it with "the Vicious Circle." Eventually they became known as "the Round Table"—a name which received wide circulation in 1920 when Edmund Duffy, a cartoonist on the *Brooklyn Eagle*, drew a caricature of the group, wearing shining armor and having lunch at a round table.

Round Table charter members included Alexander Woollcott, Dorothy Parker, Deems Taylor, Robert Benchley, Alice Duer Miller, Franklin P. Adams, George S. Kaufman, Marc Connelly and Heywood Broun. They were all smart, ambitious young people living and working in New York, all with talent, varying degrees of self-assurance and scorn for what they considered to be dull and commonplace.

The talk at the Round Table was fast-paced, sometimes witty and usually designed to hurt. When members of the group discovered something that did not match their lofty standards, they assailed it. People who talked or wrote sloppily were special objects of opprobrium. Woollcott and Adams in particular were fanatics on English usage. According to Frank Case's daughter, Margaret Case Harriman, they could spend hours arguing over the meaning of a word and woe betide the hapless person who used "who" and "whom" improperly. F.P.A would not only damn him at luncheon, but would print the error in his column, "The Conning Tower," underscoring the point with the question "Whom are you, Cyril?"

Snobs one and all, the group proclaimed to the world that they hated snobbery and any form of pretentiousness. They heartily disliked Jed Harris, the theatrical producer. He was affected, they thought, and inclined to do outrageous things simply to attract attention. Once George S. Kaufman went to Harris's office on business and was greeted by the producer seated at his desk in the nude. Kaufman didn't bat an eyelash. He said coolly, "Jed, your fly is open."

Unflappable reactions were important. Faced with misfortune, a Round Table member was expected to rap out an appropriate one-liner. Kaufman's ill-fated play, *Someone in the House*, opened during a severe epidemic of influenza. The Board of Health urged people to keep away from crowds. Seeing rows of empty seats in the theater night after night, Kaufman told his press agent that he was thinking of running an ad for the show—"See *Someone in the House*, the only place in town where you can be safe from a crowd."

At the time the Round Table started, its most distinguished member was Franklin P. Adams. His column, "The Conning Tower," which ran in the *New York Tribune* and then in the *New York World*, was considered one of the best newspaper columns in the country. Many famous writers of the day first appeared in F.P.A.'s column. Dorothy Parker credited Adams with having "raised her from a couplet," and Sinclair Lewis, Edna St. Vincent Millay and Edna Ferber were all early contributors. Adams was so sought after by literary hopefuls that he never had to pay writers for their contributions to his column. Instead he held an annual banquet at which the writer whose work had appeared most frequently that year in "The Conning Tower" was given a gold watch.

Physically Adams resembled his protégé, George S. Kaufman. Both men were tall and thin, with rather long, sad faces. "Good God," Irvin S. Cobb, the humorist, once said when he spied a moose head on the wall of a club, "they've shot Frank Adams!"

Adams was a man whose words could bite. He was once

forced to listen to a garrulous bore who finished a long-winded anecdote with the cliché, "Well, to make a long story short." "Too late," replied Adams.

At Adams's house one day, Woollcott picked up a copy of one of his own books and sighed, saying wistfully, "Now, what is so rare as an Alexander Woollcott first edition?" "An Alexander Woollcott second edition," Adams shot back.

Another outstanding member of the group was Heywood Broun, then a sportswriter on the *New York Tribune*. He was a huge man whose perpetually rumpled appearance caused one friend to remark that he looked like "a one-man slum."

At one point in his career Broun was a drama critic on the *New York Times*. Displeased by an actor's performance, he wrote that the man was "the worst actor on the American stage." The actor sued, but the case was thrown out of court. Shortly afterward, Broun reviewed a play in which the same actor appeared. Curious to know how Broun would handle the situation, his friends could scarcely wait to read his review in the morning paper. Broun nicely bypassed any mention of the actor who had sued him until the last sentence of his review. It read, "Mr. So-and-So's performance is not up to its usual standards."

An ardent crusader against social injustices, Broun once defined a liberal as "a man who leaves the room when the fight starts." He is also credited with "The only real argument for marriage is that it remains the best method for getting acquainted" and "Repartee is what you wish you'd said."

When they weren't eating lunch or tearing someone to pieces, the Round Table members played games endlessly—poker, charades, quiz games, "Murder" and croquet, which they sometimes played for ten dollars a wicket and one thousand dollars a game. Fixated on fun-with-words contests, they even competed at making up the names of fictitious law firms, such as Bright and Early, Fast and Growthin and Bold, Resolute, Gay and Berkowitz. They also liked to play the "I-can-give-you-a-sentence-game." A typical sample: "I can give you a sentence with the word 'burlesque.' For example, I had two soft burlesque for breakfast."

One of the most skilled dramatists of the day, George S. Kaufman was almost as crazy about the sentence-game as he was about bridge, excelling at both. He once stopped Frank Case in the Algonquin lobby. "Frank, I can give you a sentence with the word 'punctilious,' " he said. "I know a farmer who has two daughters . . . Lizzie and Tillie. Lizzie is all right but you have no idea how punctilious."

Always providing keen competition was Dorothy Parker, who announced: "I can give you a sentence with the word 'horticulture.' You can lead a whore to culture, but you can't make her think."

The undisputed master of these revels was Alexander Woollcott, around whom the Round Table revolved in its palmiest and most publicized phase. A crusty, enigmatic man who weighed over 250 pounds, Woollcott resembled an overstuffed owl and had a strange love-hate relationship with his friends. He would snipe at them one moment, then praise them, in his florid prose, the next. Rudeness was his trademark. He was in the habit of greeting people with such endearments as "Hello, repulsive," and when irritated might say, "I find you are beginning to disgust me. How about getting the hell out of here?" Once when he was forced to endure a long-winded anecdote told by a boring friend, he interrupted the man to say, "Excuse me, my leg has gone to sleep. Do you mind if I join it?"

Even his closest friends were not spared the inventions of his poisonous tongue. When he learned that George S. Kaufman's wife Beatrice, a largish woman, was having an affair with a man who was also on the heavy side, he remarked that "seeing them together is like watching two plum puddings in heat."

Some people seem to have been flattered by his insults. "Being noticed by Aleck at all placed you a few rungs up the ladder of success," said Russel Crouse. Certainly his influence on the world of his day was great—both as a drama critic and as the radio host of the CBS program "The Town Crier." People feared him and hated him, but the public found his carefully devised cruelties frightfully amusing and his easy sentimentality deeply moving. In the 30s, when he reigned over a world of radio fans, he was laughed at and quoted and regarded as a great wit as well as an authority on crime and literature.

As a theater critic Woollcott reviewed plays in much the same way he treated people. His style has been called "combined treacle and pure black bile." "The leading man should have been gently but firmly shot at sunrise" was an example of the underlying venom he could bring to some unfortunate actor who no doubt had been trying his best in a hopeless part.

In a flash he could turn on an actress he had once raved over. "Mrs. Patrick Campbell," he wrote brutally in a review, "is an aged British battleship sinking rapidly and firing every available gun on her rescuers."

The composer Sigmund Romberg was a favorite target. Knowing that Romberg often borrowed liberally from other composers, Woollcott noted, "The audience whistled the tunes going *into* the theater."

Alexander Woollcott was born in 1887 in Phalanx, New Jersey, a small socialistic community founded by his grandfather near Red Bank. His father, Walter, an Englishman, was a rolling stone who never stayed at any job for long, including the job of fatherhood.

Aleck hated him.

"The son of a bitch left us dangling from the brink of insecurity over the pit of poverty," he told Margaret Leech Pulitzer, the historian. "What on God's earth was there for me to love about my father? Or even admire?"

The same questions sometimes were asked by Aleck's friends about Aleck himself.

Woollcott attended Hamilton College in Clinton, New York, where he played all the female leads in the school's drama club productions. Friends remember him appearing at campus parties on occasion dressed as a woman, and according to one of his biographers, Howard Teichmann, he even had calling cards printed that read "Alexandra Woollcott."

His sexuality was the cause of much speculation during his lifetime and even after his death. Although not a homosexual, he took no pleasure in intercourse with the opposite sex. This he freely confessed, attributing his impotence to a case of the mumps he had suffered as a young man. Teichmann believes this story to be a fabrication and thinks that in all probability Woollcott—with his high-pitched voice and hips like a woman, his tendency to overweight, and his feminine temperament—suffered since birth from a hormonal imbalance, most likely an insufficient amount of the male hormone, testosterone.

Whatever his peculiarities, he learned to make the most of them—emphasizing his idiosyncrasies and caricaturing himself in a bizarre life-style that he paraded before his friends, inspiring many of them to write about it. As everyone knows who has seen the Kaufman and Hart comedy *The Man Who*

Came to Dinner, the character of the crochety, self-centered Sheridan Whiteside was a direct takeoff on Woollcott, a portrait of all his foibles and overblown conversation. Hart said he was inspired to write it after Woollcott was a guest in his home. In the course of the visit, Woollcott ordered the maids around, invited his own friends over for meals, and upon leaving, wrote in Hart's guestbook, "This is to certify that on my first visit to Moss Hart's home, I had one of the most unpleasant times I ever spent."

To his credit, Woollcott reacted good-humoredly to the play's unflattering portrait, and even played himself in several road company versions. When asked how he felt about the character of Whiteside, he replied, "Whiteside is merely a composite of the better qualities of the play's two authors, Kaufman and Hart."

He lived in an apartment on East 52nd Street which Dorothy Parker promptly christened "Wit's End." The bathroom was adorned with photos of Woollcott sitting on the toilet. At Wit's End on Sundays, he would preside at all-day brunches, dressed in rumpled pajamas and jousting verbally with friends who dropped in. He also, as time went on, became the co-owner with other Round Tablers of Neshobe Island in the middle of Lake Bomoseen in Vermont. Games and high jinks were the order of the day at both Wit's End and Neshobe. There were also elaborate jokes, which Woollcott adored, and which became even more fantastic and pornographic after his friend and protégé Harpo Marx joined the group.

Woollcott had many crushes, and Harpo was perhaps his favorite. He discovered Harpo when he saw him in *I'll Say She Is!*, clowning with his brothers. To Woollcott, Harpo was a rare talent, almost unearthly in his surrealist genius, and he raved about him, invited him to his apartment and weekend house parties, laughing at all his antics like a child with a new toy.

One weekend afternoon, while a group of Round Table members were vacationing on the island, Alice Duer Miller, a popular novelist of the time, announced that a group of tourists had dared to invade the premises. Harpo at once volunteered to chase them away. In his own words, he describes what happened. "I stripped off all my clothes, put on my red wig, smeared myself with mud and went whooping and war-dancing down to the shore, making Gookies [a Harpoism for grotesque faces] and brandishing an axe. The tourists snatched up their things, threw them into the boat and rowed away fast enough to have won the Poughkeepsie Regatta."

Another time, when Harpo and Woollcott were vacationing on the French Riviera, Woollcott invited his idol, George Bernard Shaw, to lunch. Shortly before Shaw and his wife were due to arrive, Harpo went swimming in the nude. When he saw the Shaws driving up, he jumped out of the water and covered himself with a towel. Shaw, seeing him, asked who he was. As Harpo was answering, Shaw snatched off his towel and impishly announced, "This is Mrs. Shaw."

This probably would have qualified Shaw for immediate membership in the Round Table had he sought it.

Harpo and Shaw became good friends, and Harpo spent most of that summer chauffeuring Shaw around the Riviera. When Woollcott learned of their friendship, he snapped jealously, "Harpo Marx and George Bernard Shaw. Corned beef and roses."

When one looks back on some of the Round Table frivolity, one would never think that certain people in the group ever had time to write the novels, plays and poems that ultimately made them famous. They sound much too busy being pixies and elves, or taking complicated revenge on each other, to sit at their typewriters turning out manuscripts.

The practical jokes that some of them devised often took weeks and even months to work out. People in those days went to great pains and considerable cost to amuse themselves at the expense of their friends. Even so busy a man as Harold Ross, editor of *The New Yorker*, and his first wife, Jane Grant, spent several months working up an elaborate hoax aimed at Alexander Woollcott, their houseguest. Woollcott had a portrait of himself he greatly cherished, and the Rosses had an artist paint a copy of it which was slightly askew and which they slipped into the frame of the original picture. For weeks they kept saying to Woollcott, "What on earth is happening to your picture?" Then, when he was nearly beside himself with puzzlement, they slipped the original portrait back into the frame.

One of the most celebrated practical jokes played on Woollcott was devised by Charles MacArthur, co-author of *The Front Page* and an inveterate practical joker. Woollcott hated people to be late for an appointment and when MacArthur showed up at Wit's End a few minutes late one day, Woollcott left the apartment, telling his manservant that he could wait no longer. When MacArthur arrived, he decided to get even and promptly went to the grocery store, where he purchased many packages of raspberry Jell-O. Returning to Wit's End, he asked the manservant if he could use the bathroom and then locked the door, plugged up the bathtub drain, turned on the-hot water and dumped package after package of Jell-O into the tub. He then added cold water in the proper porportions, opened the bathroom window wide to the cold night air, and stepped quietly from the room, closing the door softly behind him.

When Woollcott arrived home and found his bathtub filled

to the brim with hundreds of portions of the raspberry dessert, his only recorded comment was that he wished Charlie had made it lime, so as to match his bathroom's décor.

Woollcott died of a heart attack in 1943 and was cremated at his request. Although he had asked that his ashes be mailed to his alma mater, Hamilton College, for burial in the university graveyard, insufficient postage was put on the package and it was returned to the crematorium, lacking sixty-seven cents.

Eccentric, unpredictable and infuriating as Woollcott was, it is amazing to realize that in his day he mesmerized so many people and kept the Round Table going by the sheer force of his personality. The Round Table would not have been the same without him. One of the reasons is possibly that he cared so deeply about his little circle. He wrote about it rhapsodically, talked about it on the radio, and did his best to convince himself that the people in it were geniuses and their antics hilarious.

Although time has proved that few of the Round Table members were as great as Woollcott made them out to be, many of them, like Kaufman, Benchley and Parker, were extremely talented and produced work which is still highly regarded today. The best of their humor is still piquant and original, despite the fact that the brittle badinage and sophomoric sophistication has worn thin with the passing of the years.

It must be remembered in any discussion of the Round Table that it existed at a time when people were far less blasé than they are today, and could still laugh at outlandish practical jokes and the childish pranks of the rich and famous.

Not all their contemporaries approved of Woollcott and the Round Table. The group had many critics, who accused them of logrolling, that is, plugging somebody's book in exchange for a plug about one's own. They were also accused of writing and rehearsing their witticisms in advance.

James Thurber, the great *New Yorker* humorist, never cared for them. "All these guys, including Ross, played pranks so elaborate and long they became burdens," he wrote to Groucho Marx. H. L. Mencken avoided the lunches, even though many group members idolized him. "Mencken's lack of interest in the Round Table," Anita Loos once remarked, "had caused him to remark, 'their ideals were those of a vaudeville actor, one who is extremely "in the know" and inordinately trashy.' " And Gertrude Atherton, a novelist of the 20s, satirized them in her 1923 bestseller, *Black Oxen*. She called them "The Sophisticates," and portrayed them as "gathering at the sign of the Indian chief, where the cleverest of them—and those who were so excitedly sure of their cleverness that for the moment they convinced others as well as themselves—foregathered daily."

Edmund Wilson saw them as children of the suburbs who had been taught a kind of gentility which they were now mocking from a level of pseudo-New York sophistication. The only person in the group he found interesting was Dorothy Parker, who he felt was "naturally, spontaneously witty," yet who could "alternate effusive affection with remarks, once the object was no longer present, of a well-aimed and deadly malice."

By 1930 the group had more or less disbanded. Some of its members had left New York to work in Hollywood, and some, like Dorothy Parker and Heywood Broun, had become more interested in politics and social issues. It is hard to pinpoint just when the group ended, but fewer and fewer people were attending the one o'clock luncheons, and those who did were not of the same caliber as the bright, talented young people who had come ten years earlier. Divorces, remarriages, success and time had also changed the original founders, and they who had looked on life with an amused superior eye now realized that it could be horrible and frightening, not something to be warded off easily with a bon mot or one-liner. So . . . one by one . . . at the Round Table chairs stood empty, the luster and gaiety were gone.

2

Robert Benchley

The Kindliest Wag

"In America, there are two classes of travel—First Class and with children."

IT HAS been said that wit is aggressive by nature. Wit—more often than not—laughs at, rather than with, its object. Many wits have been angry, tormented and insecure people who used their talent to strike out at others. Yet the life and career of Robert Benchley give evidence that it is possible to be a wit and a kindly person too. Indeed, Benchley was so pleasant a man that people said his presence in a room made everyone feel better. Dorothy Parker called him one of the most delightful men she had ever met. Even John O'Hara, who was ordinarily skeptical about most of his contemporaries, wrote, "I cannot think of anyone who has not been advanced spiritually, culturally and even financially by association with Mr. B."

Robert Benchley was one of the original Algonquin wits, but his brand of humor was never malicious or aggressive. He seldom poked fun at other people's absurdities, but concentrated on describing his own fears and inadequacies when faced with the dangerous business of daily life. A Harvard graduate, a brilliant writer and a bon vivant, he nevertheless liked to portray himself as a bumbler, a vague and helpless person who was always unsure of himself in a bewildering world. His charm lay in his gentleness and air of constant perplexity. He gave the impression that no matter how hard he tried to understand it, life never made much sense. Behind this image he hid, and so successfully that very few people ever knew the real Benchley.

A portly man with a round bemused face, a small, well-clipped mustache and dark hair neatly parted in the middle, Benchley liked to say that his life was a ceaseless struggle against inanimate objects. Typewriter ribbons and cellophane wrappers seemed bent on conspiring against him. "It may be a perfectly dandy wrapper, air-tight, water-tight and germ-proof, but if the buyer has to send it to a garage to get it off, something is wrong somewhere," he once said.

Obviously he needed a secretary to help him cope with the hazards of modern life. He found one in the person of Charles MacGregor, a middle-aged Scotsman. Benchley sensed that for him MacGregor would make a perfect secretary because when they were introduced, MacGregor was holding a bouquet of flowers and told Benchley that he wasn't taking them to his mother or his sweetheart but to a shirt in the shirt hospital.

Such a man was a perfect foil for one who loved whimsy as much as Benchley—and as time went on, MacGregor showed a remarkable talent for invention in the Benchley style. One of his duties was to get Benchley out of bed every morning. In his biography of his father, Nathaniel Benchley writes that MacGregor "was a genius at waking a person gently and inoffensively. He would walk into the bedroom and say, very quietly, 'The men are here for the trunks,' and Benchley would be thrown into an immediate turmoil of activity, stumbling about the room and groping for clothes to put into the nonexistent trunks. By the time he realized it was all a ruse, he was as wide awake as a third baseman. Naturally, MacGregor didn't say the same thing every morning; he varied it with such things as, 'There are some men here to flood the bed for skating.' "

The practical joke, which has long since lost its cachet among the sophisticated, was a favorite form of humor in Benchley's day, and he was a master of it. In the 1940s, when he was out in Hollywood making a series of movie shorts, he contracted pneumonia. A doctor was sent for. He prescribed a sulfa drug, then told Benchley he would return in a few days to see how he was progressing. Benchley took the drug as ordered, and on the day that the doctor was due to call, he and a friend ripped open a bed pillow and painstakingly glued all the goose feathers inside it to Benchley's body from his waist to his toes.

The doctor arrived and, after examining Benchley, asked him if he had experieced any bad effects from the drug. Benchley said he didn't think so, although there was one minor symptom that was bothering him a bit and would the doctor mind looking at it and giving him an opinion. So saying, he tossed off the sheet, revealing the goose feathers.

His fondness for practical jokes began during his college years in Boston when he and a crony knocked on the door of an expensive house on Beacon Hill. A maid answered, and they told her they had come to pick up a davenport in the hall. Although she seemed rather confused, she allowed them to take it. After picking up the couch, Benchley and his chum carried it across the street to another expensive house. When the maid appeared there, they told her that they had brought the davenport and asked where she would like it placed. She led them to a downstairs sitting room, and after leaving the davenport, they beat a hasty retreat. "The matter wasn't straightened out for several months," Nathaniel Benchley writes, "when the owner of the davenport went to the other house for tea and recognized her property. The explanation that 'two men just left it here' was accepted graciously, albeit a little coldly."

Margaret Case Harriman, whose father was Frank Case, owner of the Algonquin, tells the story of a weekend her parents spent with the Benchleys at their home in Scarsdale. When the Cases arrived, they found every towel in the bathroom inscribed with the name Hotel Algonquin. Downstairs the cocktail shaker, the silverware, the plates and glasses were all marked with the hotel's name. The bedsheets and pillowcases were also obviously hotel property. Mr. Case could stand it no longer.

"I see you've been staying at the Commodore lately, Bob," he said.

Benchley liked to send telegrams. Once when he was in Venice, Italy, he cabled David Niven, "Streets full of water. Advise."

He also was fond of inventing imaginary biographies of himself. He summed up his life one time by saying that he was born on the Isle of Wight, September 15, 1807, shipped as a cabin boy on the *Florence J. Marble*, 1815, and was arrested for bigamy and murder in Port Said, 1817. He was released in 1820, Benchley claimed, and thereafter wrote *A Tale of Two Cities*. Married Princess Anastasia of Portugal in 1831 (children: Prince Rupprecht and several little girls). Wrote *Uncle Tom's Cabin*, 1850. Began *Les Misérables* in 1870, finished by Victor Hugo. Died 1871. Buried in Westminster Abbey.

Actually, Robert Charles Benchley was born in Worcester,

Massachusetts, on September 15, 1889, the second son of Charles Henry Benchley, the Mayor's clerk, and Maria Jane Moran. Jennie, as she was called, was an exceptionally strong-willed woman of pronounced tastes and violent prejudices. Her loathing of alcohol in any form was exceeded only by her hatred of trees—based on the fact that trees had a longer life span than she supposed she would have. When the eccentric Mrs. Benchley was still in her twenties, she had all her teeth pulled out, after one or two started giving her trouble.

Her first son, Edmund, was born in 1876. A tall, handsome boy with a whimsical sense of humor, he was her favorite child. When he was killed by a sniper in the Spanish-American War, she was heartbroken and sobbed, "Oh, why couldn't it have been Robert?" This outburst was overheard by Robert and repeated all over town.

After Mrs. Benchley pulled herself together, she was horrified by what she had said and reacted by pampering Robert inordinately.

Robert attended Phillips Exeter, where he endeared himself to his classmates by drawing cartoons and making fun of the class assignments. When told to write an essay on something practical, he turned in a paper entitled "How to Embalm a Corpse." To prepare for it, he took a few lessons from the local undertaker.

After graduation, he went to Harvard, where he became editor in chief of the *Lampoon*, the college humor magazine, and delivered the speech, "Through the Alimentary Canal with Gun and Camera." At commencement, he gave the "Ivy Oration." His speech, a morass of non sequiturs that parodied the usual academic address, was received with a standing ovation.

For a short time, Benchley considered a career in the diplomatic service. His hopes of finding employment in this profession were dashed when it came time for him to take his final exams in international law and he suddenly became violently ill with the flu. A proctor was sent to his room, where Benchley took the exam in bed. Possibly his illness affected him more severely than he realized: When asked a question dealing with the Newfoundland fishing rights dispute between the United States and England, Benchley answered the question from the point of view of the fish.

His instructor was not amused, and Benchley flunked the course.

In the spring of his senior year at Harvard, he became engaged to Gertrude Darling, whom he had known since Sunday School. She was the daughter of a prosperous businessman who owned a mill in Worcester. They were married not long after Benchley's graduation. During the first years of their marriage, he worked at a series of jobs to which he was ill-suited; he was a secretary to the director of the Boston Museum of Fine Arts, and then an advertising writer for the Curtis Publishing Company. An an advertising writer, he was always being told that his work "lacked punch," and perhaps simply to prove that he wasn't altogether humdrum, or in the spirit of his old college waggery, he donned a red wig and false beard at the annual sales convention and passed himself off as a Mr. Constantine, president of a Seattle advertising agency. When he was asked to make a speech, he seized the opportunity of lambasting the business practices of the Curtis Publishing Company to such an extent that Mr. Curtis, the president, had to be restrained from leaping to his feet and rushing to the podium. When his speech was finished, Benchley ripped off his disguise. There were titters of embarrassed laughter and then a dreadful silence.

After being fired from the Russell Paper Company in Boston, Benchley finally began working with Franklin P. Adams as associate editor of the *New York Tribune*'s Sunday magazine section. One might have thought this would have been a perfect job for a man of Benchley's talents, but apparently he was as unhappy on the *Tribune* as he had been with the Curtis Publishing Company. He rated himself "the worst reporter, even for his age, in New York." According to his son Nathaniel, "the main reason for this was that he lacked the ability, or the nerve, to ask people questions that he considered none of his business." Once when he was assigned to cover an affair at the Colony Club and was told that reporters were not permitted at the event, he returned to his desk and jotted down a description of the club's doormat. The *Tribune* did not print the piece.

But as time went on, his articles in the *Tribune* and his freelance pieces for *Vanity Fair* gained him a growing reputation as a wit and sophisticated stylist. One of the first pieces he wrote for *Vanity Fair* was called "No Matter from What Angle You Look at It, Alice Brookhausen was a Girl Whom You Would Hesitate to Invite into Your Own Home."

When the *Tribune* magazine folded, Benchley went to work as managing editor of *Vanity Fair*. It was at this time that he met Dorothy Parker, then *Vanity Fair*'s drama editor, and Robert Sherwood, its drama critic. All three soon became fast friends, although they still continued to call each other Mr. Benchley, Mrs. Parker and Mr. Sherwood. Sherwood, a quiet, slow-talking man, was six feet seven inches tall, Benchley six feet, and Dorothy Parker a petite five feet. Someone once said that seeing them walking together was like looking at a "moving pipe organ."

When Benchley was asked if he knew Bob Sherwood, he scrambled onto a chair and stretched out his fingers until they just grazed the ceiling. "Bob Sherwood? Of course, I've known him since he was this high," he answered.

At *Vanity Fair*, the trio often frittered away much of the day talking about the plays they hoped to write and thinking up ways to bedevil the management. One day a memo was circulated saying that any employee who told anyone else the salary he or she was getting would be fired. The other employees accepted this dictum. Not Dorothy and the two Roberts. They all made signs specifying their salaries, and hung them around their necks.

When another office memorandum was passed around, this one saying that anyone who was late to work must have a written excuse, Benchley reached for a piece of paper and in a microscopic scrawl explained that the reason he had been eleven minutes late for work that morning was that as he was leaving his house, he had encountered a herd of elephants which had escaped from the Hippodrome and were about to enter an ocean liner. In order to prevent a calamity at sea, he had helped round them up and return them to the Hippodrome.

When Dorothy Parker wrote an unflattering review of Billie Burke's performance in a play by Somerset Maugham, Miss Burke's husband, Florenz Ziegfeld, told the management of *Vanity Fair* that he would withdraw his advertising if Miss Parker continued as drama editor. She was fired, and both Benchley and Sherwood, who felt she had been treated unfairly, resigned in protest. Later she and Benchley shared a small office together as free-lance writers. It was so small, Benchley said, that "One cubic foot less of space, and it would have constituted adultery." Benchley's earnings as a free-lance writer were not enough to support his wife and family, and he decided to take a job as drama editor of *Life*, a weekly humor magazine whose title was later bought by the pictorial weekly.

Benchley insisted that he knew nothing about the theater or play reviewing, but soon his sprightly critical pieces began to attract a legion of admirers. One of the high points of his career as a critic was his running battle with the long-lasting play of the twenties, *Abie's Irish Rose*. When this drama of an Irish girl and a Jewish boy opened in 1922, it was universally panned. Robert also wholeheartedly damned it. The play proved to be a smash hit—and ran for the next five years. Part of Benchley's job at *Life* was to write "The Confidential Guide," a weekly one- or two-line summary of every show in town. Confronted with the task of offering a critique of a play he thoroughly despised, Benchley wrote in the first week, "Something Awful." As the play's run dragged on interminably, he began to create such desperate descriptions as "Just about as low as good clean fun can get," or "Showing that the Jews and the Irish crack equally old jokes," or "The comic spirit of 1876," or "People laugh at this every night, which explains why democracy can never be a success," and finally, "Will the Marines never come?"

Although never as caustic as Dorothy Parker or Alexander Woollcott, Benchley could demolish a play with a single phrase. He described Cosmo Hamilton's *Scandal* as "What no young girl ought to know." Of another play, he said, "It was one of those plays in which all the actors unfortunately enunciated very clearly."

One evening in 1926, while he was attending a first-night performance of *The Squall*, a melodrama relying heavily on the use of Pidgin English, he turned to his wife Gertrude and said that if he heard another word of phony Spanish dialect, he was going to leave. At this point a scantily clad, dark-eyed Gypsy girl burst onstage, and slithered on her hands and knees across the floor to the feet of the mistress of the house.

"Me Nubi," the Gypsy girl announced. "Nubi good girl. Nubi stay here."

Benchley stood up. "Me Bobby. Me bad boy. Me go," he whispered loudly.

Whereupon he and Gertrude left.

According to Nathaniel, Benchley and his wife sat behind Woollcott and an unidentified woman at the opening of *He Who Gets Slapped*. During a circus scene, "three beautiful white horses—real ones—came on, and the middle horse had its lips drawn back in a broad, toothy smile. Robert leaned forward and tapped Woollcott on the shoulder. 'See that middle horse?' he said. 'That's Violet Kemble-Cooper (Violet Kemble-Cooper was a popular actress of the time, who had a broad smile and a handsome, glistening set of teeth.)

"Woollcott gave a barely perceptible start, then turned halfway around, and looked at the woman beside him. 'Miss Kemble-Cooper, may I present Mr. Benchley?' he said, to the actress's younger sister.

"Robert swallowed, then smiled. 'But it's such a beautiful horse,' he said."

Many years later, when Benchley had given up drama criticism for a career as a radio and movie comedian, he and a friend went to a play. Before the show, they had something of a liquid lunch, and shortly after the curtain went up, Robert fell asleep in his seat. His nap was interrupted by the ringing of a telephone on stage. With a start he woke up and shouted, "Will someone please get that phone!" and then added, "It might be for me."

The next morning one of the newspaper reviews read: "Show awful, but Benchley wonderful in small part."

Upon hearing of the death of a famous Hollywood movie actress with a reputation as a nymphomaniac, Benchley suggested an epitaph: "She sleeps alone at last."

Once Benchley was staying at the home of a boring elderly aunt. She had asked him to take a walk with her one afternoon, but he demurred because it was raining heavily. A little while later she saw him sneaking out of the house. "Oh, Robert," she called, "has it cleared up?" "Just a little bit," Benchley replied. "Enough for one, but not enough for two."

And then, there was the night in Hollywood when he left the Trocadero restaurant and found that it was raining. A uniformed man was standing on the sidewalk, and Benchley went up to him and said, "When you have a chance, would you mind calling me a taxi?"

"I'm not the doorman," the man said irritably. "I'm an admiral in the U.S. Navy."

"Sorry," Benchley answered. "Well, in that case, would you mind calling me a battleship?"

During Benchley's years as a drama critic, he began to write books, which he characterized as "being riddled with pitfalls for sanity." Among these early works were *Love Conquers All* (1922), *The Early Worm* (1927), and *20,000 Leagues Under the Sea, or David Copperfield* (1928). In 1920 and 1921, he also wrote a column, "Books and Other Things," which ran in the *New York World.*

In 1922, he appeared in *No, Sirree!*, a revue written and acted by the Algonquin wits for a selected group of friends. Many well-known entertainers and artists appeared in this show (the offstage music was provided by Jascha Heifetz). Benchley's skit was entitled "The Treasurer's Report." He conceived of it in a taxi on the way to rehearsal, and it was an inspired mishmash of mutilated figures and mixed metaphors. When Benchley delivered his skit, the audience adored it. Irving Berlin was so impressed by Benchley's acting that he asked him to perform the skit in his *Music Box Revue*. Benchley agreed, and several weeks on Broadway followed, with "The Treasurer's Report" placed early in the show so he could leave to review other plays for *Life*.

In 1929, Benchley left *Life* to become drama critic for *The New Yorker*. He also wrote "The Wayward Press," another *New Yorker* column in which, under the pseudonym of Guy Fawkes, he criticized the New York newspapers. In this same year he also began a movie career by filming "The Treasurer's

Report" as a short subject. Audiences were tickled by his incomprehensible financial calculations and his self-deprecating little chuckle. During the course of his life, he would make forty-eight of these shorts for various film companies. Among his better-known film shorts are *The Sex Life of the Polyp, How to Vote, How to Sleep* and *How to Raise a Baby*, all of which he described as "Benchley humiliations recollected in tranquility."

Although Benchley enjoyed his job as *The New Yorker* drama critic, there was one part of the job he hated, and that was having to turn his copy in on time. The mere mention of the word "deadline" upset him. Benchley wrote slowly, and as soon as he finished a piece, immediately found fault with it. Nathaniel recalls that his father confessed to him that "it took me fifteen years to discover that I had no talent for writing, but I couldn't give it up because by that time I was too famous." He often missed deadlines. Then waggishly he would send the editor a telegram, with some fantastic explanation as to why the piece was late. Or else he would get his mother (who still lived in Worcester, Massachusetts) to send a wire signed by him, saying that the reason his copy was late was that his mother was ill, and he had to go to Boston to be with her till she recovered. As time went on, the content of these telegrams became more and more fantastic, and it was almost as though Benchley were sending the wire not as an excuse but simply to amuse and entertain his friends. He was living up to their conception of him, accommodating his style to an image he had created. Instead of appearing at a luncheon he did not want to attend, Benchley had his mother wire his hosts the following message, signed with his name: "Sorry, I can't attend luncheon today because I am in Boston STOP. Don't know why I am in Boston, but it must be important because here I am."

Once somebody told Art Samuels, editor of *Harper's Bazaar* and one of the recipients of a "mother-is-sick" telegram, that he had seen Benchley at a New York hotel only a couple of hours before. Then, realizing his blunder, he called Benchley and apologized for what he had done. According to Nathaniel, "immediately Benchley started sending telegrams to friends all over the country, and after an interval collect telegrams signed with his name began to trickle and then to pour into the *Harper's Bazaar* office, saying that he was in Santa Fe being inducted into a Navajo Indian tribe, that he was in Florida judging the Orange Blossom Carnival, that he was in Detroit inspecting the new Packard engines, that he was in Hollywood working on a picture with Greta Garbo, and that he was in Maine acting as a guide for a hunting party. Only the fact that the telegraph company refused to send collect cables from Europe kept him from having been in London, Chantilly and Rome. Finally, at the end of the day, a telegram arrived for him collect, from Samuels. It said, simply: "I GATHER YOU HAVEN'T DONE THE PIECE."

While Benchley was working for *The New Yorker*, he decided to move to the Royalton Hotel, which was not far from the magazine's offices. For years he had lived with his wife and two sons, Nathaniel and Robert, Jr., in Scarsdale, New York, but now he thought it more practical to spend the week in town and go home on weekends. At first he had tried living at the Algonquin, but finding that he was distracted by friends dropping by his room and inviting him to poker games down the hall, he moved across the street to the Royalton. Here he maintained a small apartment which soon grew incredibly cluttered. Its room overflowed with Victorian furniture, photographs of Queen Victoria at various stages of her life, deer skulls, a stuffed two-headed calf, old newspapers, busts of Sir Walter Scott and bookshelves full of odd reading material including *The Culture and Diseases of the Sweet Potato* and *In and Out with Mary Ann*. There was also his typewriter, and a dilapidated blue couch which Benchley called "the track," saying as he lay down on it for a nap, "Well, it's time for a couple of laps around the track."

The most frequent visitors to Benchley's rooms were pigeons, which he despised. They alighted on the window ledge outside his bedroom every morning and woke him up with their incessant cooing. Benchley considered all birds his natural enemies. Once while he was staying at the Garden of Allah, he looked out his bungalow window and thought he saw a bird he described as being a cross between a flamingo and a seagull. Muttering, he ran out of his room and tried to punch it. "Everyone ought to see a bird slip on its tail at least once," he wrote. "It is a gratifying experience and good for the soul." In one of his pieces he described a blackbird whose flying struck him as amatuerish.

Benchley once left a note for the milkman at Grant's Tomb. It was stuffed into an empty milk bottle and said, "One milk, no cream, U. S. Grant." A lifelong champion of disorder, he loved to create confusion and would purposely mix up appointments and write notes to his bank on the back of his checks, such as "Dear Banker's Trust. I love you, Bob" or "Having a wonderful time. Wish you were here. Robert Rabbit Benchley." Once he applied to his bank for a loan and received it. The next day he withdrew all his savings. "I don't trust a bank," he explained, "that would lend money to such a poor risk."

All his friends had a favorite story to tell about him; how he valiantly tried but never really mastered the art of using an airplane seat belt; how he hated being thought of as an intellectual and would slip a dust jacket of a murder mystery over his copy of Proust; how he always read footnotes and when they referred to another work, would not continue his reading until he had found and read the book referred to. When a tobacco company asked him about his favorite brand of cigarettes, he replied, "Marijuana." He is reported to have rung up the late ex-Kaiser of Germany at his retreat in the Netherlands after feeling a sudden urge to converse with someone in German. Once when he was very young, he had a heated argument about Lillian Russell's attributes with a policeman's horse. This one-sided conversation drew a rather large crowd.

Benchley, however, never invented the quip which has been regarded as his most famous: "Let's get out of these wet clothes and into a dry martini." His son says it was a line which appeared in someone's column and that a press agent attributed it to Benchley.

The son of a mother who hated alcohol, Benchley was a teetotaler all through Prohibition. After being persuaded to have a drink, however, he made up for lost time by drinking inordinately. His capacity was huge. He would start drinking at five in the afternoon and keep on until the early morning.

After he moved into the Royalton, Benchley's nightlife became more and more riotous. Although deeply devoted to his wife and family, he had many extramarital affairs, mainly with actresses. He was a regular customer at Polly Adler's, a well-known bordello in New York, where he would sometimes finish his magazine pieces. According to Babette Rosmond, author of *Robert Benchley: His Life and Good Times*, "Benchley often said that his best articles were written at Polly's, or as he pronounced it, Pawly's. One naive young lady always thought Benchley was talking about visiting a suburban family when he said, 'Let's all go to Pawly's'—something he said quite frequently."

Two of his favorite places to go as he grew older were Tony's, a speakeasy owned by Tony Soma, and "21," where there is still a plaque over his favorite table, inscribed with the words "Robert Benchley, His Corner 1889–1945."

There was a dark side to Benchley, but it was part of his credo never to show it. He merely had another drink and tried to think of something funny to do or say.

Yet, as time went on, this bonhomie wasn't always possible. Edmund Wilson in his journal describes an evening spent with Benchley and Dorothy Parker in New York which gives a painful picture of Benchley's increasing alcoholism and lack of self-control at this period of his life. Wilson writes:

" 'Do you mind going up to Tony's?' (It was inevitable that she should insist on going to one of their regular hangouts; they didn't know how to get along with anybody but one another.) 'Mr. Benchley is sunk tonight, and I promised I'd go up there and see him.' (It was one of their affectations that she always called him Mr. Benchley)—His girl and awful little whore, unfaithful to him, made him give her money (Mrs. Benchley busy with children's tonsils), he was getting worse and worse in debt (his syndicate stuff began to show it—overdrafts on Scarsdale bank), he would rush out to Chicago, where the mistress was playing, to lecture; the girl had been a waitress, then on the stage, he had met her in *Music Box Revue*; he would say, 'She enters the room like a duchess!'—When I finally met her, she was quite a pretty blonde with thick ankles, who, however, I thought, had something of that hard-eyed prostitute stare, the result of there being no coherence or purpose in a woman's emotional life.—We drank a great many Tom Collinses. When we first came in, we had found Benchley, with his red grossening face, leaning against the wall in the hall—talk of going down to the cellar to sing—

he had got to a point where he no longer went at all to the plays he reviewed for *Life* . . ."

In 1943, at the age of fifty-four, Benchley announced that he was quitting as a magazine writer and was going to concentrate on radio and movie work. He felt that very few humorists excelled in their work as they got older and he was afraid he was beginning to lose his comic touch. Although his short films were highly successful, he gave up his writing career with sadness. He once told Dorothy Parker that "each of us becomes the thing he most despises," and now, it seemed he was doing that very thing. Years after Benchley's death, Robert Sherwood told his son about seeing Benchley at a Hollywood party. Nathaniel Benchley writes:

"At one point, late in the evening, Benchley was heard to say, 'Those eyes—I can't stand those eyes looking at me!' Everybody stopped and turned, and saw that Benchley was backing away from Sherwood. They waited, already smiling and set to laugh at the joke that was about to come, but Benchley was serious. He pointed at Sherwood and said, 'He's looking at me and thinking of how he knew me when I was going to be a great writer. . . . And he's thinking *now* look at what I am!' "

Benchley continued to stay in Hollywood, making shorts and playing character parts in thirty-five feature films, including the role of a society drunk in *China Seas* (with Clark Gable and Jean Harlow), a harried newspaperman in Alfred Hitchcock's *Foreign Correspondent*, and Shirley Temple's father in *Kiss and Tell*. He was given carte blanche to write his own part in these films. He also wrote several books of short pieces, such as *Inside Benchley* (1942) and *Benchley Beside Himself* (1943). But his new career was still not satisfactory to him. As Nathaniel Benchley says, his father "didn't really want to be funny; what he wanted more than anything else was to be a good writer, and he was frustrated because the only way he could make money was as a comedian. He summed up his dilemma to Harold Ross, editor of *The New Yorker*, by saying, 'I'm not a writer and not an actor. I don't know what I am.' " His major ambition was to write a history of the Queen Anne period, and until the time of his death he was still collecting books to be used as source material for his proposed work. But Benchley no longer seemed to have the energy for creative work, and as Nathaniel wrote, "it depressed him that he no longer seemed to care. The sleeping pills that he took at night kept him awake, and the Benzedrine that he took on the movie lot made him drowsy, and he finally gave up taking the Benzedrine because he could think of no particular reason for wanting to stay awake anyway."

When he died in 1945 of a cerebral hemorrhage, his friends held two separate memorial services—one in New York at "21," the second at Romanoff's in Beverly Hills arranged by his longtime friend, Dorothy Parker. Toasts were drunk, and anecdotes were told. It was the kind of wake he would certainly have wanted. For when the humorist George Ade had died many years before, Benchley had remarked, "When a great humorist dies, everybody should go to a place where there is laughter, and drink to his memory until the lights go out."

3

George S. Kaufman

The Wits' Wit

"The trouble with incest is that it gets you involved with relatives."

EVEN AMONG the Algonquin wits, most of whom could be counted on to be one another's severest critics, George S. Kaufman was considered one of the most brilliant and funny men of his time. Not that George outwardly gave any indication of this distinction. Tall and dour, with a bushy black pompadour and dark eyes peering funereally over rimless spectacles, he looked like a frightened crane. He was shy and hypochondriacal and would often walk along the street talking to himself and making faces. Yet in the course of his long life, he wrote hit comedy after hit comedy and invented many bons mots which were quoted all over town. He also managed to find the time to conduct innumerable love affairs with pretty women, including a well-known movie star.

Kaufman's wit was usually delivered in a deadpan manner. "Satire is what closes on Saturday night," he once said. At a party one of the guests told him he had found a new play on Broadway so exciting he had seen it three times. "What's the matter?" Kaufman asked him. "Didn't you get it the first time?" Puns and other forms of wordplay were his stock-in-trade. "One man's Mede is another man's Persian," he remarked at a poker game. Of an actor named Guido Nazo, he said "Guido Nazo is nazo guido." And then afraid that Nazo's career might suffer as a result of the quip, he called up friends in the theater until he found one who might offer Nazo a part.

Unlike some of the other Algonquin members who wisecracked incessantly, Kaufman doled out his witticisms an inch at a time. In the course of an afternoon he might utter only one sentence, but it would invariably be fresh and on target. One of his most quoted remarks was inspired by a guest who spent the lunch hour tracing his family back to the Crusades. Kaufman, who despised snobbery, could stand it no longer. "I too had a famous ancestor," he said quietly, "Sir Roderick Kaufman. He also went on the Crusades." His voice grew softer. "As a spy, of course."

On another occasion, Raoul Fleischmann, the yeast heir who helped finance *The New Yorker* in its early years, confessed to Kaufman that he was fourteen years old before he knew that he was Jewish.

Kaufman replied, "That's nothing. I was sixteen before I knew I was a boy."

Although he admired her clever, inventive mind, Kaufman regarded Dorothy Parker with something less than enthusiasm. "Everything I've ever said will be credited to Dorothy Parker," he grumbled. He also found her habit of swearing and her tendency to make off-color jokes unladylike and unattractive.

Kaufman was a Jew and Parker half-Jewish. One day at the

Round Table, Woollcott—who liked to play at being a bigot—yelled at Kaufman, "Shut up, you Christ-killer!" In the silence that ensued, Kaufman rose from his place and announced to the assembled company, "I will not stay here and listen to any more slurs on my race. I will not stay here and be a captive audience of Mr. Woollcott and his vile pronouncements. I am now leaving this table and the Algonquin." After making this statement, he looked hard at Dorothy Parker, who had said nothing, and was still sitting there. "And I hope that Mrs. Parker will follow me—halfway."

Possibly the most versatile talent in show business in his day, Kaufman not only coauthored forty five plays, of which twenty six were hits, including the Pulitzer Prize-winning *Of Thee I Sing* (1931) and *You Can't Take It With You* (1936), but was an accomplished director, actor, play doctor, screenwriter and drama critic as well. Yet in spite of the fact that his plays were usually smashing successes, he was always convinced that his next one would be a failure. Opening nights caused him to turn pale with fright. He said he felt "a little like the late Marie Antoinette in a tumbrel." On the opening night of *Dulcy,* his first successful play, he was so nervous during the performance that he paced up and down the center aisle of the theater, causing the play's producer to ask, "Who is that drunk in the audience?"

Kaufman wrote most of his plays with collaborators. Among them were Edna Ferber, Morrie Ryskind, Moss Hart, Ring Lardner and Herman Mankiewicz. A perfectionist, he often spent hours polishing a sentence, or an entire afternoon discussing an exit line. Moss Hart dubbed their first collaboration "The Days of Terror." Kaufman's behavior as a creator almost drove Hart crazy. In fact, the act of playwrighting seemed to spark Kaufman's restless nature, and he would pace the apartment, plucking imaginary pieces of lint from the furniture, opening and closing venetian blinds, and picking up Hart's letters and personal belongings, examining them absentmindedly, then casting them aside. This behavior so irritated Edna Ferber, with whom he collaborated on *The Royal Family*, (1927) that she planted a telegraph blank face down among the letters on her desk. While seeking the perfect exit line for one of their characters, Kaufman began rummaging through her belongings. He picked up the telegraph blank and read: "George Kaufman is an old snoop."

Having honed a line to perfection, Kaufman objected violently when it was tampered with. In his mind, the worst offenders were the Marx brothers, who were compulsive adlibbers and liked to treat their audience to a new show every night. During a rehearsal for *The Cocoanuts,* a musical comedy Kaufman had written for them, Kaufman nudged a spectator and whispered, "I thought I just heard one of my lines."

Groucho, however, was vastly impressed by Kaufman's comic talent—"He gave me my walk and my talk," he later admitted—and eventually persuaded his brothers to play *The Cocoanuts* pretty much as written, at least at first. Later Groucho made an attempt to stick in a few of his own jokes and justified it by saying, "They laughed at Fulton and his steamboat, too." Kaufman was not impressed. "Not at matinees," he retorted.

The actor William Gaxton was also given the Kaufman treatment when he began improvising on the script of *Of Thee I Sing.* At intermission, Kaufman, who had dropped by to see the show incognito, left the theater and went to the nearest Western Union office, where he sent a telegram to Gaxton: "Am sitting in the last row. Wish you were here." He sent another telegram to an actor who aspired to become a playwright. "Your performance magnificent and improving every day. Sorry I can't say same about lines."

In fact, Kaufman mistrusted actors in general, even when they delivered their lines correctly. A determined foe of pomposity and conceit, he couldn't stand celebrities who were inflated with their own success. The actor Raymond Massey was famous for his interpretation of Abraham Lincoln and eventually began to live the part, adopting Lincoln's style of speech, even his mannerisms and dress in private life. Kaufman sneered, "Massey won't be satisfied until somebody assassinates him."

Charles Laughton, fresh from his triumph as Captain Bligh in *Mutiny on the Bounty*, once bragged to Kaufman that it was easy for him to play Bligh because many of the men in his family had been outstanding seafarers. Recalling the actor's portrayal of Quasimodo in *The Hunchback of Notre Dame*, Kaufman remarked, "Then no doubt you also come from a long line of hunchbacks."

George S. Kaufman was born in Pittsburgh, Pennsylvania, on November 16, 1889. Of his Jewish family he said, "They managed to get in on every business as it was going bankrupt and made a total of $4 among them." His mother, Henrietta, a tall beautiful woman, became emotionally disturbed after the death of her second child, Richard, who died at the age of seven and a half months. When young George was born three years later, she pampered him excessively and insisted that he was much too delicate to participate in sports. All the milk and water he drank had to be boiled, and he was kept away from people who were sick, from lakes and swimming pools and heights. George grew up to be a man plagued by a number of obsessions and phobias he was never able to overcome. All his life he avoided physical contact and cringed if someone touched him or if he was forced to shake someone's hand. He had a hand-washing fetish and never touched a doorknob with his bare hands for fear of germs. His diet during the latter years of his life consisted of meat, bread, chocolate mints and fudge he made himself. He loathed vegetables.

A confirmed hypochondriac, George was convinced that he suffered from a fatal illness. Until the end of his life, he was morbidly afraid of death.

Kaufman was an intensely private man who discouraged intimacy with his collaborators and theatrical associates. He is believed to have had only one close friend. "I truly believe that the only person who ever caught more than glimpses of Kaufman was George Kaufman himself," James Thurber wrote, "and it is a pity that he did not put himself on paper in an autobiography, but it is also unimaginable that he would have done so." The producer Max Gordon felt that George deliberately shut people out. "And if he did not succeed with his eyes or manner," Mr. Gordon said, "he did so with his rapier wit which he used so effectively off-stage and on."

Perhaps some of Kaufman's phobias sprang from a tragedy which occurred in his childhood. Shortly after the birth of her fourth child, his mother developed symptoms of hysteria. She would suddenly clutch her chest, begin gasping for breath and tell George to fetch a doctor. The other family members learned to take these episodes calmly, but little George felt they were serious and tried to help his mother as best he could. Howard Teichmann, one of Kaufman's biographers, felt that these scenes were so upsetting to the child "that when the time came for him to write true emotion, he quickly hid behind a joke. What insights he might have had as a serious playwright were forbidden to come to the page. He had all the emotionalism he wanted as a boy . . ." It is a well-known fact that whenever a love scene was called for in one of his plays, Kaufman refused to write it and gave the task to one of his collaborators.

It may also be that George, a professional wit, had no interest in lines which did not reveal his true talent.

When Kaufman was eighteen, his father got a job as a superintendent of the Columbus Ribbon Mill in Paterson, New Jersey, and moved the family there. For a while Kaufman worked in the ribbon factory as a ribbon and hatband salesman, but spent most of his spare time inventing puns, jokes and quips which he sent in to Franklin P. Adams's column, "Always in Good Humor," in the *New York Evening Mail.* Adams signed his column "F.P.A.", and Kaufman signed his contributions "G.S.K." Adams was impressed by his work and published most of his offerings.

One day he invited his young contributor to lunch. Impressed by the thin, gawky young man still in his teens, Adams recommended him for a job on the Washington *Times.* From 1912 to 1913, Kaufman wrote a column called "This and That and a Little of the Other" for the newspaper. It was more or less an imitation of F.P.A.'s column in the *Evening Mail.* The column was a success, and Kaufman might have remained with the paper forever if Frank P. Munsey, the owner, had not walked into the city room one day and spied Kaufman. "What's that Jew doing in my city room?" he shouted. Within minutes George was fired. Again F.P.A. came to his rescue. As he was leaving the *Mail* for the *Tribune,* he recommended George for his former column on the *Mail.* Kaufman's new column was called "Be That As It May" and ran for only a year. He then worked as a reporter on the *Herald Tribune* and eventually became a drama reporter for that paper. When the job of first-string drama critic became vacant and an unknown sportswriter named Heywood Broun was given the post, George quit the *Tribune* and went to work for the *New York Times.* He spent thirteen years at the *Times* as drama editor, quitting his job during the Depression only because he felt that with so many people out of work someone who needed the money should have the job. By that time, he was a highly successful playwright, with money from royalties pouring in each week and producers clamoring for his services.

As a reviewer, Kaufman was generally kindly, although he maintained some rigid rules. He would not print any item about a play a friend of his was involved in, nor accept any publicity handout sent to him by a press agent. "How do I get our leading lady's name in the *Times*?," a press agent asked him. "Shoot her," barked Kaufman.

"There was laughter in the back of the theater," one of his reviews began, "leading to the belief that someone was telling jokes back there." To a fellow dramatist, he said, "I understand your play is full of single entendres." Another work was dismissed with the quip, "I saw the play at a disadvantage. The curtain was up." At the opening of a bad play, he reportedly tapped the woman sitting in front of him and said, "Madame, would you mind putting your hat on?"

The drama section of the *Times* used to run as a service to its readers a feature which by means of daggers, asterisks and other special symbols dispensed information on all the current plays. Deciding that the column had grown unwieldy, Kaufman found a new symbol in the composing room and slapped it in front of the title *Strange Interlude*, Eugene O'Neill's tragic drama, which ran for almost five hours, straight through the dinner hour. The maze led to a footnote reading "Does not carry dining car."

While he was a *Times* drama critic, Kaufman wrote a farce entitled *Going Up*, which was never produced, even though he rewrote it thirty-five times. Actually, *Going Up* was not his first attempt at drama. At the age of fourteen he had written a play entitled *The Failure*, a melodrama about a self-sacrificing father whose son is a disappointment to him. It was produced at a community playhouse in Pittsburgh. As for *Going Up*, it was not an utter loss. John Peter Toohey, the press agent who took Woollcott to lunch and started the Algonquin Round Table, liked its dialogue and recommended Kaufman to the producer George C. Tyler, who needed someone to rewrite the comedy *Among Those Present*. Kaufman did the rewrite, but the play was not a success. Tyler then hired Kaufman to rewrite another comedy, *Someone in the House*. This too was a flop.

About this time Kaufman met Marc Connelly, a reporter for the *Morning Telegraph*, and the two men collaborated on *Dulcy*. They borrowed the central character, Dulcinea, from F.P.A.'s column, where she appeared frequently as a dispenser of clichés and bromides. The playwrights' spoof of middle-class boredom and big business enchanted the audience, and Kaufman and Connelly became two of the most popular playwrights of the 20s.

Two more hits in 1922, *To the Ladies* and *Merton of the Movies*, were followed by two failures the following year: These were *Helen of Troy, New York* and *The Deep Tangled Wildwood*. But the collaborators made a comeback in 1924 with *Be Yourself* and *Beggar on Horseback*.

Beggar on Horseback was the last play Kaufman wrote with Connelly. Although they separated amicably and continued their friendship until Kaufman's death, their professional relationship had been a strain. Kaufman told Howard Teichmann that Connelly's work habits and his own were not compatible. Kaufman liked to start work early in the morning and seldom stopped for meals or sleep, often getting up in the middle of the night to polish a scene. Connelly was relaxed and casual. He would show up late for work, or might not come at all. "But he always had an excuse," Kaufman said. "Margalo Gillmore always had a dead cat to bury, or someone was always arriving and had to be met. Or someone was always sailing and a bon voyage party was being held aboard ship. Finally, I told him, 'Marc, someday New York harbor will freeze over, and you'll write the best damn play anyone's ever seen. It didn't, but he did." That play was *The Green Pastures*, which the critics praised as the best play of the 1929–30 season and which won a Pulitzer Prize.

Connelly's easygoing attitude toward writing bothered Kaufman, who felt that Connelly was wasting his talent. In the middle of one of Connelly's prolonged spells of non-writing, a lost manuscript of Charles Dickens's *The Life of Our Lord* was discovered and published. Kaufman used the occasion to prod his old collaborator: "Dickens writes more dead," he said to Connelly, "than you do alive."

After writing two more hits entirely on his own, *The Butter-and-Egg Man* (1924) and *The Cocoanuts* (1925) for the Marx brothers, Kaufman went back to collaborating with other writers. Among them were Edna Ferber, with whom he wrote *Dinner at Eight* (1932) and *Stage Door* (1936), and Moss Hart, with whom he wrote *Once in a Lifetime* (1930), *You Can't Take It With You* (1936), and *The Man Who Came to Dinner* (1939), "an unexpurgated version of Alexander Woollcott." Kaufman was also a play doctor, skillful at fixing up the work of other writers. When one of his own plays was not up to snuff, he would remark, "What this play needs is George S. Kaufman."

Kaufman was also an excellent director. It was he who directed Ben Hecht's and Charles MacArthur's *The Front Page*, John Steinbeck's *Of Mice and Men*, and *Guys and Dolls*, one of America's greatest musicals. As a director, Kaufman hated any interference with his work. Frank Loesser, the composer of *Guys and Dolls*, told him that he would like to include a reprise of songs in the second act. Kaufman answered, "If you reprise the songs, we'll reprise the jokes."

When he wasn't writing or directing plays, Kaufman loved to play poker and bridge. He excelled at both games. Saturday nights usually found him at The Thanatopsis Pleasure and Inside Straight Club, an offshoot of the Algonquin Round Table, playing poker all night long with Marc Connelly, Robert Benchley, Heywood Broun, Herbert Bayard Swope, Harpo Marx, Alexander Woollcott, and Harold Ross. One night the group was joined by Charlie Chaplin, whose new film, *The Gold Rush*, had just opened in New York. In those early days of his career, Chaplin was as poor a conversationalist as he was a poker player. The only subject he talked about was his blood pressure.

"I went to my doctor last week," he told the group, "and he told me my pressure is down to 108."

"Common or preferred?" Kaufman said without looking up.

One night he had the misfortune to have a very poor bridge partner. After they had played a hand, the partner, sensing that he had made several frightful mistakes, asked Kaufman plaintively, "How would you have played it?"

"Under an assumed name," Kaufman replied.

During another bridge game with another wretched player, Kaufman's partner got up and said he was going to the men's room. "Okay," Kaufman nodded, "at least this is the first time this afternoon I'll know what you have in your hand."

As compulsive about his bridge playing as he was about playwrighting, Kaufman once stopped a game to say, "I'd like a review of the bidding with the *original* inflections."

One of the poker players at the Thanatopsis club was a sedate young theatrical press agent named David Wallace. He was a favorite of the group because unlike the other Algonquinites, he was content to listen rather than compete and try to steal the limelight. David was popular among them for another reason; he was the perfect butt for many of their practical jokes. His middle initial was H, and for some reason nobody could find out he did not want people to know what it stood for. After several attempts to find out the truth, Kaufman and other members of the Round Table began sending in bad jokes to *The New Yorker*, all credited to David H. Wallace. These jokes were always pointless or feeble or old hat. "It, quoth David H. Wallace, gnomic graybeard, 'never rains, but it pours.' " Or, "As David H. Wallace says, 'Tea and coffee are good to drink, but tennis is livelier,' " or "David H. Wallace, the monologuist, convulsed his set with a good one the other evening. 'It seems there were two Irishmen,' Mr. Wallace began, but could not go on for laughing.' " Years later Wallace told Margaret Case Harriman that only once did Kaufman credit him with a real joke. He recalled it with a shudder. "It raised my hair," Wallace told Mrs. Harriman. The "joke" was "Once there were two Jews, and *now* look."

Although kind and considerate in general, Kaufman irrationally hated cab drivers and waiters and waged a lifelong battle against them. He once composed an epitaph for a waiter: "God caught his eye." The only thing that he hated more than a pokey cab driver or an indifferent waiter was someone who insisted on arguing with him in a cab over who should pay the fare. In the hope of averting such arguments, he kept a roll of one-, five- and ten-dollar bills in his pocket so that as soon as the cab reached its destination, he could whip out the money before his fellow passenger could protest that it was his turn to pay.

Kaufman's friend, Harpo Marx, thought this obsession was idiotic and resolved to cure him of it. "I cut a small hole in my pants pocket and stuffed the pocket with bills," he recalled.

"George and I shared a taxi from Woollcott's house to the Algonquin. When we got to the hotel I jumped out of the car, opened my fly, reached in, pulled out a five-spot and handed it to the driver. There was quite a crowd around the hotel entrance, and I had a good audience. George was too mortified to speak. He slunk out of the cab, red-faced, praying that nobody would recognize him."

Kaufman was timid in public and making him blush was one of Harpo's favorite pastimes. Once, when they were having dinner on a train, an old lady was seated opposite them. She finished her dinner before they did, and asked for her check. The waiter brought it on a little silver tray. Before she could pick it up, Harpo reached over, grabbed the check, put salt and pepper on it, then ate it. Kaufman was so embarrassed that he writhed in his chair. "When he was acutely discomfited," Harpo said, "he would try to wind his right arm twice around his head and reach back to his right ear."

That same weekend, while Harpo was at the Kaufmans' farm in Bucks County, Pennsylvania, playing croquet on the lawn, the game was interrupted by the arrival of two Quaker ladies who had come to ask Beatrice Kaufman, George's wife, about doing some charity work. Mrs. Kaufman took her guests inside, telling Harpo and George that she would be out in a few minutes. When she did not return on time, George went to look for her. "He went inside to rescue Beatrice from the Quakers," Harpo recalled. "Twenty minutes passed. No Beatrice. No George either. Now I was getting edgy. I looked in the window. There sat both the Kaufmans, cozily sipping tea with the ladies from the Society of Friends. I went to the kitchen and dumped a bottle of ketchup down the front of my shirt and pants. I went to the doorway of the living room, where I stood, dripping ketchup.

" 'Excuse me, Ma'am,' I said, addressing Beatrice. 'I've killed the one cat, and he'll be ready for dinner, but I still haven't caught the other one. Will one be enough?'

"The visitors departed in haste, and our game resumed. Beatrice couldn't stop laughing over the Quakers' retreat, but George was practically reduced to ashes. He couldn't get his ball through another wicket and never did make it to the stake."

Beatrice Kaufman was the former Bea Bakrow of Rochester, New York. She and Kaufman were married when he was twenty-eight. She was not a beautiful woman. Her figure was on the heavy side, her complexion was poor, and she had dark kinky hair parted in the middle. Most people found her charming, however, and very attractive. She was always beautifully dressed, and she was passionately interested in people. A trendsetter, she wore slacks long before they were stylish and was psychoanalyzed in a period when few people went to analysts. Bright and fiercely independent, she had gone to Wellesley College but was expelled for leaving a sedate tea to go for a drive with a perfect stranger. He turned out to be none other than Enrico Caruso, a notorious womanizer.

Although Beatrice was not beautiful, many distinguished men loved and admired her. Alexander Woollcott and Oscar Levant found in her a wit that afforded them many a chuckle. "I once took Beatrice to Carnegie Hall to hear Stokowski conduct Bach's B Minor Mass," Oscar Levant recalled many years later [like her husband, Beatrice hated good music]. "We were late. 'In heaven's name, let's hurry,' said Beatrice, 'or we'll miss the intermission!' "

Beatrice was engaged to a rabbi when she and George met on a blind date. As soon as she listened to Kaufman's conversation, she forgot all about the rabbi, and soon she and Kaufman were engaged. In spite of her parents' opposition (they considered George a struggling young newspaperman with no future), the couple were married on March 15, 1917, in Rochester. At the end of their first year of marriage, Beatrice was pregnant. Nine months went by, and still she did not deliver. Finally labor was induced. The infant, a boy, hopelessly deformed, was stillborn.

After this sad event, the Kaufmans' sex life deteriorated seriously. One biographer has said that after the child's death, George became impotent whenever he attempted intercourse with his wife, theorizing that when Beatrice became pregnant, she became associated in his mind with his mother and sleeping with her was tantamount to incest. Another biographer thought it was Beatrice who curtailed their sex life. For her, sex had ended in agonizing emotional and physical pain, and she could not bear the thought of another abnormal pregnancy. Still she loved George deeply and wanted to remain his wife.

What is certain is that the Kaufmans remained married for twenty-eight years and obviously had an extramarital arrangement. Each one had many affairs, Beatrice with a number of influential men, George with perhaps hundreds of actresses and chorus girls. Most of these affairs were full of sincere emotion on his part, and the women he paid court to continued to adore him, even after the relationship had broken up. According to reports, Kaufman was a marvelous lover. He was tender, considerate, always showering his girlfriends with gifts, writing them ardent love letters and giving them money when they needed it. Even after his lady loves married someone else, he kept in touch with them and was upset if he heard their lives turned out unhappily.

Of his many liaisons, the most publicized was with Mary Astor, the famous beauty and movie star whom he met in 1934. Born Lucile Langhanke in Quincy, Illinois, she was a tall, auburn-haired woman with a face of classic refinement.

When she and Kaufman met in New York, she was still married to Dr. Franklyn Thorpe, a successful Hollywood physician. They had one child. But domestic affairs bored her—and so did Dr. Thorpe, who seemed more interested in going on hunting trips with his friend, Clark Gable, than in staying home with his wife. She decided to fly East, and during the course of this trip began keeping a diary. It contained not merely her feelings and impressions, but a detailed account of her many amorous escapades. Fittingly, she wrote the details of these love affairs in lavender ink. In her diary, she wrote about her meeting with Kaufman in the following words: "I fell like a ton of bricks—as only I can fall—it was just one of those things." The affair continued on and off for a year. She seems to have been deeply in love with Kaufman, while George, according to the diary, was not as serious about his feelings for her. Although undeniably stirred by her physical attributes, he evidently felt about her as he had felt about countless other attractive women and was not prepared to risk his marriage to Beatrice on her account. "I wish I were madly in love with you, but those things just can't be arranged," he reportedly told her. "I haven't been in love for many years, and I doubt very much if I can again ever."

Shortly after they began seeing each other again in Hollywood, where Kaufman had gone to write *A Night at the Opera* for the Marx brothers, Dr. Thorpe called on Kaufman and said he knew about the affair and that "George must be willing to take his share of the responsibility involved." He thereupon left the apartment without saying another word.

In 1935, Dr. Thorpe sued Mary Astor for divorce. He was given custody of their child as well as valuable securities and real estate.

The following year, the actress asked her attorney to reopen the case. Dissatisfied with the settlement she herself had agreed to, she wanted the divorce overturned, and an annulment granted instead. She also wanted custody of their child, the real estate, and the securities. Outraged, the doctor countersued. Producing her diary as evidence of her adulterous behavior during their marriage, he began leaking the more lurid portions of it to the newspapers. Not since the Fatty Arbuckle case of 1922 had the world been treated to such a juicy Hollywood scandal. Reported *Time* magazine in its August 17, 1936, issue: "However, no screen lover but a sad-eyed dramatist was cast as Mary Astor's No. 1 partner-in-sin . . . Browsing through the diary, her husband's lawyers found that she had recorded experiencing 'a thrilling ecstasy' in the company of George S. Kaufman. 'He fits me perfectly,' she wrote, recalling 'many exquisite moments . . . twenty—count them, diary, twenty . . . I don't see how he does it . . . he is perfect.' "

Dr. Thorpe's lawyers called Kaufman as a witness, but the dramatist failed to appear in court, and a bench warrant was issued for his arrest. Fleeing from the sheriff's deputies, Kaufman at first sought refuge at the home of his collaborator, Moss Hart. Then, he was smuggled aboard a yacht owned by Irving Thalberg and Norma Shearer and taken to the island of Catalina. When the deputies discovered his whereabouts in Catalina, he sailed back to the mainland, again hiding at the Hart home. When the deputies knocked on the door, he fled across the street and hid in a neighbor's shubbery. The next day, disguised as an accident victim, with his face swathed in bandages, he was put on a stretcher and carried on board a train bound for New York. Before the train reached New York, he sneaked off at a nearby stop, where a friend picked him up and drove him to the home of his sister Ruth in New York City.

The newspapers had a field day over the affair and the Keystone Kop hide-and-seek chase Kaufman had indulged in.

Headlines about Miss Astor and "Public Lover #1," as Kaufman was called, were splashed on the front pages all over the country. Eventually, Kaufman returned to Hollywood and apologized to the judge for fleeing the authorities. Charmed by his soft speech and witty remarks, the judge fined him five hundred dollars, and all charges were dropped. The case officially was at an end.

But for George and Beatrice Kaufman, who had adopted a baby daughter (Anne) by then, the episode was traumatic. For a shy, sensitive man like Kaufman, the publicity had been agony; worst of all was his awareness of the suffering it had caused his wife, whom he loved and had always tried to protect. As for Beatrice, she was deeply shaken and humiliated by the scandal. She had tolerated her husband's extracurricular affairs, but the Mary Astor liaison was a different matter. It had not been handled discreetly, it had been made into a carnival by the press, and the entire world now knew that she and her husband were not the happily married, respectable couple they had always pretended to be. She tried to convince herself that she did not care. Superficially, she behaved as cheerfully as before, but as Ira Gershwin's wife Lee told Howard Teichmann, her friends could tell she was playing a part. "She was gay, adorable and heartbreaking. Her personal life was always with her, and even in her gaiety you could sense the hurt."

At the age of fifty-one, she died suddenly of a cerebral hemorrhage, and after that Kaufman's misery became particularly pronounced. He carried her picture with him wherever he went, and though not a religious person, burned a *yahrzeit* candle in her memory for twenty-four hours on every anniversary of her death. For the next six years, he saw few people and had little zest for work. The two scripts he worked on during this period—*Park Avenue*, (1946) a musical with Nunnally Johnson, and a play, *Bravo*, (1948), with Edna Ferber—were failures.

In 1948, some of his depression lifted when he met Leueen MacGrath, a pretty blonde English actress. They were married a year later. He was nearly sixty; she was thirty-five. At first the marriage was a happy one. Kaufman seemed to turn from a discontented, withdrawn person into an amiable extrovert. Always fearful of plane travel, he suddenly amazed everyone by flying to the South of France with Leueen for a vacation. Although he had always said he hated animals, Leueen persuaded him to buy a Siamese kitten, and he fell in love with it. He even went shopping with his stunning new wife, something he had refused to do with Bea. Once when he and Leueen were looking at drapery fabric in Bloomingdale's, a salesman approached and asked if he could help him. "Yes," Kaufman said thoughtfully. "Do you have any good second-act curtains here?"

Soon after his second marriage, his energy and creativity seemed to have returned. He directed several plays, among them *Guys and Dolls*. It was a resounding success, but shortly after it opened, he suffered a stroke. When he recovered, he and Leueen tried collaborating on several plays. The only one they wrote that succeeded was the musical *Silk Stockings*. Its reviews were good, but the experience was marred by constant clashes between the Kaufmans and the producers Cy Feuer and Ernest Martin.

As in his first marriage, Kaufman eventually became unable to have sexual relations with his wife, and Leueen, an attractive, healthy woman in her forties, began dating other men, including the producer Carmen Capalbo and Dorothy Parker's estranged husband, Alan Campbell. The Kaufmans were divorced in 1957.

During the 50s, Kaufman appeared frequently on a TV

show, "This Is Show Business," created and produced by Irving Mansfield. During the holiday season, the panel was asked what they would most like for Christmas. "Let's make this one show on which nobody sings 'Silent Night,' " George promptly replied. Immediately the station was deluged with calls from irate listeners, and Kaufman was fired from the show. But his fans protested, and he was eventually rehired. Several years later when he was old and bedridden, he created quite a stir when he telephoned the announcer of a radio show playing semiclassical music. During the request hour, the announcer had been taking calls from people requesting various selections but few pieces of music were played to the finish, and most came to an abrupt end after merely a few bars. Too feeble to get out of bed to turn off his radio, Kaufman desperately phoned the number the announcer had given his listeners.

"Are you really George S. Kaufman?" the announcer asked excitedly, after the playwright had introduced himself.

"Yes," Kaufman said. "I am *the* George S. Kaufman."

"Well, sir, what is your request? I'll honor it right away."

"My request," Kaufman said over the air for all to hear, "is for five minutes of silence."

It was his last public performance. He had long suffered from arteriosclerosis and began to have a series of small strokes. Increasingly, his mind wandered. Once he was found walking along Park Avenue, wearing only his bathrobe. Leueen abandoned her acting career temporarily so that she could take care of him. But sick as he became he never quite lost his ability to turn a clever phrase. Toward the end of his life, he ran into an old friend, Peggy Leech Pulitzer, who was about his age. "My God, Peggy," he cried. "I thought we were both dead."

As he grew feebler and frailer, he lost his fear of death. "I'm not afraid anymore," he told Leueen and his daughter Anne once after awakening from a deep sleep. He died on a summer morning in 1961 at the age of seventy-two. At his funeral, the eulogy was delivered by his friend and collaborator Moss Hart, who said: "There were many Georges. There was George the cantankerous croquet player, irritable and implacable, a marvelous loser but a poor winner. There was George the terror of headwaiters, taxi drivers, and barbers—yet strangely, almost foolishly sentimental. There was G.S.K. the wit, certainly one of the wittiest men of his time, always genuinely surprised that his own special way of life should be considered witty. There was a wintry and distant George, but there was also a warm and springlike George, though not everyone saw this side of him, for he was not always a comfortable man or what we think of as a cozy man. Yet, and this was the contradiction, he was a loving man. It might surprise him to hear me say that, but he was . . ."

4

Dorothy Parker

"Little Nell and Lady Macbeth"

"One more drink and I'd be under the host."

SHE WAS a mass of contradictions, and no two people who knew her could ever agree on what she was really like. Dorothy would embrace someone warmly, murmuring endearments and eternal devotion, then as soon as the person's back was turned, say something cruel about him or her. Although a charter member of the Round Table, once it disbanded she did her best to debunk it, lambasting herself and her fellow members for not being more concerned about social issues. "Dammit, it was the twenties, and we had to be smarty. I *wanted* to be cute," she said. Yet, although she later downgraded her reputation as a wit, every reporter who came to interview her was greeted with a fresh set of quips.

A small, fragile brunette with thick brown bangs and an air of disarming helplessness, Dorothy Parker was one of the most talked about women of her time. Her short stories appeared at regular intervals in *The New Yorker* and *The Bookman*, and her collection of verse, which ranged from poetic lyrics to short humorous rhymes, were bestsellers. In 1927, under the pseudonym "Constant Reader," she began to write a book review column for *The New Yorker*. Two years later, she was awarded the O. Henry Prize for "Big Blonde," a corrosive story about a former party girl of the twenties who after separating from her husband sinks into alcoholism and suicidal despair.

She was also the queen bee of the literati who met each day for lunch at the Algonquin. During the late twenties and thirties, almost every smart comment that circulated through New York was attributed to Dorothy Parker. Many she did not invent and had no connection with. But as she said in her later years, "Why, it got so bad that people began to laugh before I opened my mouth. A 'smart-cracker' they called me, and that makes me sick and unhappy. There's a hell of a distance between wisecracking and wit. Wit has truth in it, wisecracking is simply calisthenics with words."

In her day, Dorothy was a master at word calisthenics. Hearing that a well-known English actress, famous for her love affairs with members of the legal profession, had broken her leg, she cracked, "She must have done it sliding down a barrister." One day, a woman writer came up to Dorothy at the Round Table and began to brag about how long she had been married and what a wonderful man her husband was.

"I've kept him these seven years," the lady enthused.

"Don't worry," Dorothy replied. "If you keep him long enough, he'll come back in style."

Dorothy Parker said of Katharine Hepburn, who was appearing in the play *The Lake*, that she ran "the whole gamut of emotions from A to B." Later she took another pot shot at Miss Hepburn, who at that point in her career got so nervous before she went on stage that she had the stagehands construct a special passageway from her dressing room to the wings so she would see no one who would distract her from concentrating on her lines. Miss Hepburn's co-star in *The Lake* was the distinguished actress Blanche Bates. When Dorothy Parker heard about the passageway, she said, "That's to prevent Katharine Hepburn from catching acting off Blanche Bates."

Of Margot Asquith's autobiography, she wrote in *The New Yorker* that "the affair between Margot Asquith and Margot Asquith will live as one of the prettiest love affairs in all literature," adding that Miss Asquith's book was in four volumes, "suitable for throwing."

In another *New Yorker* review she damned A. A. Milne's children's book *The House at Pooh Corner* with the phrase, "Tonstant weader fwowed up." Milne never forgave her. Neither did playwright Channing Pollock, whose play *The House Beautiful* she dismissed with the one-liner, " 'The House Beautiful' is the Play Lousy." Reviewing evangelist Aimee Semple McPherson's autobiography, *In the Service of the King*, she wrote, "With the publication of this [her book], she has replaced Elsie Dinsmore as my favorite character in fiction." Of Theodore Dreiser's *Dawn* she wrote, "Nearly six hundred sheets to the title of 'Dawn'; God help us one and all if Mr. Dreiser elects to write anything called 'June Twenty-first.' " Of *Beloved Infidel*, Sheilah Graham's book written in collaboration with Gerold Frank about her relationship with F. Scott Fitzgerald, she said, "They not only dug up his bones, but they gnawed on them."

To her friends Robert Benchley and Lillian Hellman, she suggested some epitaphs they might put on her tombstone: "If you can read this, you've come too close," "This is on me," and "Excuse my dust." When she was in Paris, she met two lesbians who were considering getting legally married. She listened to them argue the pros and cons of such a union and then said in a gentle voice, "Of course you must have legal marriages. The children have to be considered."

She once sent a telegram to a woman who had just borne a child after droning on tediously for nine months about her pregnancy. "Congratulations, Mary, we all knew you had it in you." Of girls who attended the Yale prom, she speculated, "If they were all laid end to end, I shouldn't be at all surprised."

Another of Dorothy's favorite targets was the writer Clare Boothe Luce. Told that Mrs. Luce was always kind to her inferiors, Dorothy asked, "But where does she find them?"

Dorothy once went to a party where she collided with a chorus girl, also a guest. The girl stepped back and gestured to Dorothy to go ahead. "Age before beauty," she said with a smirk. "And pearls before swine," snapped Dorothy in reply, as she swept on through the door. For years this encounter was supposed to have taken place between Dorothy and Clare Booth Luce—but Mrs. Luce says that her sole meeting with Dorothy was at the home of a friend, and nothing of the sort happened.

Dorothy had the habit of resting her hand lightly on one's arm as she spoke and blinking her bright dark eyes. She was "a spare speaker," her talent resting in the precise words she chose to make a withering point. Her voice was always honeyed and soft. The deceptive air of girlish innocence was heightened by her clothes—big picture hats, long feather boas, and dainty little shoes with bows. Quite nearsighted, she never wore her horn-rimmed glasses in public or in the company of a man. She was seldom seen without a small cuddly lap dog trailing beside her.

"A combination of Little Nell and Lady Macbeth," Woollcott said in summing her up.

Dorothy terrified and enraged people. According to her

biographer John Keats, her tongue was so poisonous that many of her friends hesitated to leave the room for fear of what she might say about them in their absence. Condé Nast once ran into Dorothy in the Algonquin lobby and told her that he was going on a cruise and wished she would come with him. "Oh I wish I could," she exclaimed, looking at him soulfully. Then as soon as he was out of earshot, she murmured to her companion, "Oh God, make that ship sink!"

Another time when she was spending the weekend at the home of a friend in the country, she and another woman guest went into their hostess's bathroom. On the sink was a dilapidated toothbrush. "What on earth do you suppose she does with it?" asked the other woman. "I think she rides it on Halloween," said Dorothy.

Her self-appraisal was no more kindly than the judgments she passed on others. At a dress rehearsal of her play *Close Harmony*, which she wrote in collaboration with Elmer Rice, she sat next to the producer, Arthur Hopkins. The leading lady was highly voluptuous, and at one point during the run-through Mr. Hopkins asked Dorothy, "Don't you think she ought to wear a brassiere in this scene?"

"God, no," Dorothy answered despondently. "You've got to have something in the show that moves." And then she fled from the theater and never saw the play again. Although favorably received by the critics, it was a failure at the box office.

It was said of Dorothy by her admirers that at heart she was a sentimentalist, a romantic who wished the world measured up to her dreams. Her friends said that her cynical attitude was merely a masquerade. Underneath all the malice, she loved flowers, dogs, and a good cry.

She was born Dorothy Rothschild in 1893 in West End, New Jersey, the daughter of a Scotswoman and a Jew. Her father was a successful businessman in the garment industry. Dorothy was born two months prematurely, "the last time in my life I was early for anything." Her mother was middle-aged when she was born and died when Dorothy was an infant. The little girl hated her father. "A dreadful character," she called him, recalling that when she was late for dinner as a child, he would beat her on the wrists with a spoon. "On Sundays he'd take us on an outing," she told the late writer Wyatt Cooper. "Some outing! We'd go to the cemetery to visit my mother's grave—all of us, including the second wife. That was his idea of a treat."

She had no use for her religious stepmother and refused to call her "mother" or "stepmother." Instead, she referred to her as "the housekeeper." According to John Keats, she seldom mentioned her family.

After being expelled from a convent school where she had declared "the Immaculate Conception was spontaneous combustion," Dorothy became a student at Miss Dana's School in Morristown, New Jersey. Soon after her graduation, her father died, and she had to go to work. Frank Crowninshield, the editor of *Vogue* and *Vanity Fair*, bought some of her verses and gave her a job on *Vogue* at ten dollars a week. Here she began to write captions for the fashion department—"Brevity is the Soul of Lingerie—as the Petticoat said to the Chemise" and "This Little Pink Dress will win you a Beau" were typical.

In 1917 she married Edwin Pond Parker II, a wealthy stockbroker. "I married him to change my name," she quipped, but she was obviously in love. The honeymoon was short-lived. Edwin Parker had a serious drinking problem which grew worse as Dorothy became more successful, writing verse and dramatic criticism for *Vanity Fair*. Hoping to break his habit, Parker moved to Connecticut. He felt that away from the New York speakeasies it would be easier to cure his addiction. He asked Dorothy to come with him, but she loved New York, her exciting job, and her circle of friends and chose to stay in Manhattan. They were divorced in 1928.

Dorothy took up residence in a one-room apartment on 57th Street with a dog and a canary she called Onan because, she said, he spilled his seed on the ground. The tiny apartment was devoid of any personal touches, furnished only with bare essentials, like a hotel room, but Dorothy liked it that way, saying there was enough room in it "to lay a hat—and a few friends."

She was an inept housekeeper and told people that she couldn't boil water or turn on an appliance. Once when she was spending the night at a friend's, she ate raw bacon for breakfast because she had no idea how to cook it.

At *Vanity Fair*, she shared an office with Robert Benchley and Robert Sherwood, both relative newcomers to the magazine. According to Dorothy, Frank Crowninshield didn't know what to make of his new employees. "Mr. Benchley and I subscribed to two undertaking magazines," she later told a reporter, "*The Casket* and *Sunnyside*. Steel yourself: *Sunnyside* had a joke column called 'From Grave to Gay.' I cut out a picture from one of them, in color, of how and where to inject embalming fluid, and it hung over my desk until Mr. Crowninshield asked me if I could possibly take it down. Mr. Crowninshield was a lovely man, but puzzled."

When Dorothy was fired from *Vanity Fair*, Benchley resigned in protest. They set up shop as free-lance writers on the third floor of the Metropolitan Opera Studios. Here they did little work and continued some of the antics they had indulged in at *Vanity Fair*. For two otherwise sophisticated people, some of their public antics were flagrantly sophomoric. Riding to the Algonquin, for example, Dorothy liked to stick her head out of the cab and scream, "Help, help, this man is abducting me!" while Benchley tried to gag her with his muffler.

In the Algonquin tradition, they spent a good deal of time inventing names for their newly formed partnership, such as "Utica Drop Forge and Tool Co., Robert Benchley, President, Dorothy Parker, President." They discussed ordering stationery printed with the cable address "PARKBENCH."

When Benchley gave up free-lance writing to become the drama editor of *Life*, Dorothy became so lonely she threatened to put a sign over her door reading "MEN."

The relationship between Parker and Benchley aroused considerable speculation during their lives and even after their deaths. Some people thought they were lovers, but others who knew them well insisted their relationship was strictly platonic. Edmund Wilson, who came to *Vanity Fair* as a manuscript reader shortly after Dorothy was fired, wrote: "Dorothy regarded him [Benchley] as a kind of saint."

Certainly Wilson himself was not attracted to Dorothy. Although he found her complex personality interesting, he was repelled by the perfume she wore. "The hand with which I had shaken hers kept the scent of the perfume all day," he complained. "Although she was fairly pretty and although I needed a girl, what I considered the vulgarity of her too-much perfume prevented me from paying her court."

Other men found her desirable. Among them was Charles MacArthur, with whom she had an affair until she found out that he was dating other women (he would later marry the actress Helen Hayes). Dorothy really loved MacArthur and she took their break-up badly. She began dating other men and had to have an abortion. Then she slashed her wrists. This was the first of many suicide attempts, although characteristically she disparaged it with a joke. "May I have a flag for my tent?" she is reported to have asked, poking her head out of an oxygen tent. When she got out of the hospital, Dorothy began drinking heavily, something she had never done before. As she grew older, she also began using tuberose perfume, a scent undertakers use to mask the odor of a corpse.

Her suicidal feelings were reflected in many of her poems, particularly "Résumé":

Razors pain you;
Rivers are damp;
Acids stain you;
And drugs cause cramp.
Guns aren't lawful;
Nooses give;
Gas smells awful;
You might as well live.

"She was on the verge of tears most of the time," says William S. Targ, former editor-in-chief of Putnam's. "She did not seem to trust people's feelings for her. Bennett Cerf once wrote a warm and affectionate profile, yet when I asked her what she thought of it, she responded with a four-letter word. She simply couldn't believe that anyone could like her."

At one point, Mr. Targ approached Dorothy with the idea of writing a book on contemporary women poets. She would be the ideal person for such a project, he thought. They met frequently during the next year to discuss the book, and during their conferences, Dorothy always assured him that she was working hard on it. Once, when he was at her apartment, she pointed to a piece of paper in her typewriter and said, "That's for you." She wouldn't let him read what she had written, however, and on subsequent occasions, when he insinuated that she wasn't working on the book, she became indignant. Mr. Targ said that he never saw a line of the proposed work and came to the conclusion that she had been lying when she told him that she was working on it.

For a long time after her suicide attempt, Dorothy was unable to settle down to any one man. "I require only three things of a man," she said. "He must be handsome, ruthless and stupid." And then to prove that she meant what she said, she proceeded to have affairs with men whose only talent consisted of making her life miserable. "Her taste in men was, indeed, bad, even for writer ladies," recalled Lillian Hellman. "She had been loved by several remarkable men, but she only loved the ones who did not love her, and they were the shabby ones. Robert Benchley had loved her, I was told by many people, and certainly I was later to see the devotion he had for her and she for him. She had had an affair with Ring Lardner, and both of these men she respected, but never attacked—a rare mark of feeling—but I don't think she was in love with them, because respect somehow canceled out romantic love (she talked far too much about how men looked—handsome, well-made and so on)."

Dorothy was often seen in the company of male homosexuals. "Good fairies" were needed to take care of her, she wisecracked to friends. One night, on a lark, she and a young actor, Alan Campbell—whose sexual preferences were ambiguous—visited the Bowery to be tattooed. Shortly thereafter, they were married. He was twenty-nine. She was forty, only twelve years younger than the bridegroom's mother Hortense, with whom Dorothy did not get along. "She is the only woman I know who pronounces the word 'egg' with three syllables," she said.

She and Alan quarreled frequently, and Dorothy openly referred to her husband as "the wickedest woman in Paris." Still, it was Alan Campbell who took care of her and, according to John Keats, "kept her living and working."

At forty-two, one of her dreams became a reality. All her life she had wanted a child. Now she was pregnant. She began to knit booties and tiny sweaters. But her happiness was short-lived. In the third month of pregnancy she miscarried. Deeply depressed, she stopped writing, gained a good deal of weight, and found fault with Alan incessantly.

They were divorced but eventually remarried and moved back to Hollywood, where they continued to collaborate on screenplays. In the 1930s they received screen credit for at least fifteen films, including *Sweethearts* (with Nelson Eddy and Jeanette MacDonald), *Here is My Heart*, *Mary Burns*, *Fugitive* and *A Star is Born* (with Janet Gaynor and Fredric March).

Dorothy, like Benchley, hated Hollywood. Even her large salary as a screenwriter was not compensation for living there, she felt. "Sure, you make money writing on the Coast, and God knows you earn it," she said. "But the money is like so much compressed snow. It goes so fast it melts in your hand."

During the late 1930s she became an ardent supporter of left-wing causes. Her zeal as a reformer was eventually responsible for the deterioration of her friendship with Benchley, who found her political preaching tiresome. She was stunned and miserable when in 1945 she heard that he had died. "Isn't it a bit presumptuous for us to be alive now that Mr. Benchley is dead?" she said.

The year before, in 1944, she had stopped writing poetry. Later, she explained why she had turned her back on this important aspect of her talent to an interviewer. "I was following in the exquisite footsteps of Miss Edna St. Vincent Millay, unhappily in my own horrible sneakers. Let's face it, honey. My verse is terribly dated—as anything once fashionable is dreadful now."

In 1951, the House Un-American Activities Committee branded her "a Communist," and although she denied the charge, it cost her and Alan, who disagreed with her politics, their screenwriting careers. Two years later, she collaborated with Arnaud d'Usseau on *The Ladies of the Corridor*, a play about the bleak lives of women living alone in a small hotel in the East Sixties. (Separated from Alan once more, Dorothy was living alone at the Volney Hotel, off Madison Avenue in the East Seventies.) The play was not a success.

Alan was living with her again when he died. After an evening of heavy drinking, he and Dorothy had taken sleeping pills and the next morning, when she woke up and tried to rouse him, he was dead. She was desolate, although as usual she tried to conceal her feelings with a bitter joke. A gossipy neighbor whom Dorothy disliked had rushed over to the small bungalow in Hollywood to offer her condolences.

"What can I do to help you?" the woman asked.

"Get me a new husband."

The woman was not amused. "What a cruel and unfeeling thing to say," she said angrily. "Alan's dead for only a few hours."

Dorothy regarded her coolly. "So sorry," she said. "Then be a dear and run down to the corner and get me a ham and cheese on rye and tell them to hold the mayo."

Without Alan her life seemed to have no purpose. In frail health, she moved back to New York.

Her drinking increased and her literary output stopped altogether. She seemed to have lost her desire to live. "If I had any decency, I'd be dead," she told an Associated Press reporter who came to interview her at the Volney on her seventieth birthday. "Most of my friends are." She died at the hotel of a heart attack in 1967, a woman as complex and mysterious in death as she had been in life. Although Dorothy had complained bitterly about financial difficulties in her last years, the police found four uncashed checks in a bureau drawer, including one for $10,000. She left her entire estate to the National Association for the Advancement of Colored People, with a special bequest of $20,000 to the Reverend Martin Luther King, a man she had never met.

In her last days, she totally repudiated the pseudosophistication she had set such store by in her youth. As far as she was concerned, there was "nothing memorable" or noteworthy about the people who had been members of the Algonquin Round Table. "People romanticize it," she told the Associated Press reporter. "It was no Mermaid Tavern, I promise you. These were no giants. Think of who was writing in those days—Lardner, Fitzgerald, Faulkner and Hemingway. Those were the real giants. The Round Table was just a lot of people telling jokes and telling each other how good they were. Just a bunch of loudmouths showing off, saving their gags for days, waiting for a chance to spring them. 'Did you hear about my remark?' 'Did I tell you what I said?' . . . There was no truth in anything they said. It was the terrible day of the wisecrack, so there didn't have to be any truth, you know . . . So many of them died. My Lord, how people die."

5

Oscar Levant

The Knave of Insolence

"I'm a controversial figure; my friends either dislike me or hate me."

BY THE LATE 30s and 40s most of the wits of the Algonquin Round Table had gone their separate ways, but their tradition of irreverence was still being carried on by a sallow, sulky-looking young pianist and composer named Oscar Levant. Oscar became a national celebrity when he was chosen as one of the panelists on a popular radio quiz show, "Information Please." There he fascinated audiences with his incredible musical memory (he could identify a composition after hearing only a few notes) and his wearily insolent humor, but long before that he had been known in New York as a man whose brand of humor was on a par with his virtuoso piano playing. The waiters at Lindy's, the denizens of Broadway, and the habitués of Carnegie Hall—all knew about Oscar and his deadly ability to go straight for the jugular vein. He was an established and skilled ad-libber and quipster long before the world of radio and movies discovered him.

One of his most famous targets was the beautiful and much married Hungarian actress Zsa Zsa Gabor, of whom he said, "Zsa Zsa not only worships at the Golden Calf, she barbecues it for lunch. And she is the only lady who ever left the Iron Curtain wearing it." He also said of her, "Zsa Zsa has discovered the secret of perpetual middle age." The conductor Leonard Bernstein was also subjected to Oscar's relentless tongue-lashings. "Leonard Bernstein has been disclosing musical secrets that have been well-known for over four hundred years . . . He uses music as an accompaniment to his conducting." In one of his autobiographical books, Levant apologized for tearing Bernstein apart, but pointed out that at least he did *not* reveal "how he [Bernstein] used to play records of applause from his concerts. After all, I met Lenny eighteen years ago. I remember thinking then: Here is a young man who bears watching. Close watching."

Many other hapless celebrities came under Oscar's eagle eye. He said of Perry Como that "his voice comes out of his eyelids," of Debbie Reynolds that she was "as wistful as an iron foundry." He nominated Elizabeth Taylor as "the Other Woman of the Year." Madame Nhu was "the Sandra Dee of South Vietnam. If I were cast on a desert island with her, I would quickly make friends with the natives."

Oscar didn't spare himself either. "There is a thin line between genius and insanity. I have erased that line," he said. When he and Truman Capote, the writer, were discussing integration, Oscar confided to Capote that he was "for disintegration, personal disintegration," elaborating this statement further in *The Memoirs of An Amnesiac*. "Today I'm a neurotic basket case. My health is so bad that I may be the next premier of India." (Groucho Marx said of Oscar's memoirs, "Anybody who doesn't like this book is healthy.")

Oscar said he gave up reading "because it took my mind off myself." And it was Oscar who popularized the old Jewish witticism defining ***chutzpah*** (Yiddish for unmitigated gall). "Chupzpah is the quality which enables a man who has murdered his mother and father to throw himself on the mercy of the court as an orphan."*

"The worst thing about having a mistress is those two dinners you have to eat," he once said.

When Oscar and Bernard Herrmann, the movie composer, were discussing the first four bars of Beethoven's Fifth Symphony, which every conductor interprets differently, Herrmann asked, "How would *you* play them, Oscar?"

"I'd omit them," Oscar replied.

Marriage, Oscar said, was "a triumph of habit over hate" and "happiness [was] not a thing you experience but something you remember." He later regretted having made this second definition, which he felt was too sugary inasmuch as the *Reader's Digest* reprinted it.

More aphorisms by Oscar—On women's movies: "Where the wives commit adultery throughout the movie and at the end of the picture their husbands beg for forgiveness." On egomania: "What goes in one ear—and stays there." On ballet: "The fairies' baseball." On a good husband: "A man who is unattractive to other women." On newsreels: "A series of catastrophes ending with a fashion show." On a farceur: "When a man is caught in someone else's wife's bedroom, and when he's caught, he makes witty remarks."

His advice to young pianists was to "marry a rich woman."

Integrity, he said, "is a lofty attitude assumed by someone who is unemployed." And he added, "Imitation is the sincerest form of plagiarism."

*This wisecrack has also been attributed to the nineteenth-century American humorist Artemus Ward, among others.

Once on his television show, Oscar said, "An atheist is a man with no invisible means of support."

During his Army physical, a psychiatrist asked him, "Do you think you can kill?"

"I don't know about strangers," he replied. "But friends, yes."

Levant's candid butchering of his friends and acquaintances resulted in any number of feuds. By his own admission he lost four or five friends every time he opened his mouth. Milton Berle, Mae West and Rosalind Russell were only a few of the luminaries he insulted. All were inclined to look the other way if Oscar happened by. And with just cause. When Jerry Lewis was on Levant's television show, Oscar asked him, "Who is your favorite comedian?" "Milton Berle," Lewis replied. "Oh—you aim so high," Oscar sneered. As for Miss Russell, he announced that Warner Brothers was going to do a movie of his life and that she was going to play him. Later he compounded the cruelty by saying that she was too masculine and assertive for the role.

Billy Rose was asked if he thought Oscar had mellowed with success. "Sure," he replied, "Oscar has mellowed like an old pistol."

Oscar, who liked to refer to himself as "the intellectual equivalent of Elvis Presley," was fired from a California television show for making sneering remarks about Richard Nixon, who was then Vice President. " We have had the age of the common man," he had said on the program. "Nixon embodies the age of the commonplace man."

Another time he was suspended by executives at KCOP, a Los Angeles television station, for insulting Philco, the sponsor of his 90-minute talk show. Oscar's attractive wife June usually did the commercials, but one day she was ill and could not appear, so Oscar told Philco he would do them himself. Knowing his reputation for blasting anyone and anything, the Philco people refused the offer and hired a local beauty contest winner in June's place. When this girl came on the air, Oscar insulted her and did not allow her to do the commercial. A few minutes later, he announced to the audience, "Philco has canceled sponsorship of the show. Philco is a first-class product . . . but don't buy Philco products until they return to the show." Oscar was suspended indefinitely by the station's general manager "for inexcusable conduct on the air by a star personality." But his fans raised such a storm of protest that he was rehired the next day.

Oscar Levant's wit was not contrived. It seemed to spring from a psyche tormented by anxieties and fears. A man of super-sensitive emotions, he collected eccentricities the way some men collect stamps. Of Oscar, the noted playwright S. N. Behrman said, "He was a character who, if he did not exist, could not be imagined."

Levant was extraordinarily superstitious. The number 13, for instance, could never be uttered in his presence. He preferred to sleep on a cot in his dressing room at a concert hall rather than stay in a luxurious hotel suite which happened to be on the 13th floor. The word "death" was also forbidden—as was anything connected with it, such as wills, undertakers, hearses and graves. A well-known radio producer once came to Oscar's apartment to escort him to a show on which Levant was to be a guest. "We've found some of your old wisecracks," the producer said, "and are going to play them for you tonight to see if you remember them."

"Where did you find them?" Oscar asked the man.

"In the NBC morgue," the producer replied.

Oscar turned pale. "If you say that word to me again, I'll never speak to you as long as I live," he whispered hoarsely.

The word "lucky" he considered bad luck. So was the name

of his hometown, Pittsburgh. And the names of his parents and brothers. Flowers were out of the question. He never let his wife June wear a corsage or any kind of flower nor would he countenance cut flowers, particularly roses, in his house. Flowers, he explained, reminded him of a former sweetheart named Rose who had died in her teens. If Prokofiev's Third Piano Concerto was mentioned, he would flee the room in panic. He never wore a hat because he was sure it would bring him misfortune.

A man of violent excesses, Oscar drank forty to sixty cups of coffee a day and at night swallowed at least three sleeping pills to counteract the insomnia that sixty cups of coffee had no doubt induced. Although he adored baseball and knew all about the game, he abhorred all forms of physical exercise. "My favorite exercises are groveling, brooding and mulling," he said.

Above all things, he loved to brag about his aberrations. "I'm a study of a man in chaos in search of frenzy," he boasted.

Such a man, of course, was a natural for psychoanalysis. It soon became another obsession to add to his long list. "I recall some of the youngsters in my old neighborhood who studied law and medicine. But after thirty-five years of psychoanalysis I can safely say that I was the only one who studied to be a patient," he said.

On the air, in his later years, he was always talking about analysis and its benefits, and liked to refer to "my West Coast analyst" and "my East Coast analyst." Once he refused to be interviewed by a writer until he had made an appointment with his "East Coast analyst" to enable him to get over the disturbing effect of the interview.

He was not always a good patient. A psychiatrist once told him that his wit sprang from deep hostility. Oscar retorted, "You're hostile, but I've noticed you have no wit."

Oscar was the last of four sons born in Pittsburgh to an Orthodox Jewish family who owned a jewelry store. He joked that as an infant he ran away from home twice. This was possibly based on the fact that his mother nagged him a good deal. Annie Levant was desperately anxious that he be successful, like his three older brothers—so anxious, in fact, that years later, when he told her he'd gotten married, she said, according to Oscar, "That's nice, did you practice the piano today?" His father Max was also a stern taskmaster. Once, during a disagreement over the selection of a musical encore, he struck young Oscar across the face. "I was constantly reminded of the scholarly achievements of my older brothers," Oscar wrote many years later, "and my next to oldest brother was my father's favorite."

In high school Oscar regarded himself as stupid and unattractive. He was awarded a lemon by his classmates for being the school's worst dancer. He never forgot the insult, and as a grown man banned lemons from his house. Over-sensitive and insecure, painfully shy yet driven to succeed, Oscar as a youth was often left with the feeling that nothing he did was ever good enough. The rigid musical standards that his parents had set for him remained with him all his life—and though, as an adult, he composed an excellent piano concerto, he decided it wasn't as good as Beethoven's and never wrote another one. Later he composed a number of popular songs, but stopped writing them, too, because he felt they didn't compare to the music of George Gershwin.

"Oscar was incapable of pursuing one subject to its ultimate limits because he had so many other ways of diversifying himself, and in a way, of creating opposition within himself," says Irving Kolodin, the music critic and Oscar's collaborator on his first book, *A Smattering of Ignorance*. "He always thought of himself vis-à-vis the ultimate in any particular area that he was able to work. He had the impulse to be a serious composer but he began to study with Arnold Schönberg and that ruined him because he couldn't function on the same level with Arnold Schönberg. So that every form of impulse that he had ran into obstacles because he was aiming to exceed or excel on some very high level, and it wasn't working."

When Oscar was sixteen, his father died, and he dropped out of high school and came to New York to study music. His ambition was to be a pianist and composer like his idol, Sergei Rachmaninoff. The teachers he found were excellent; he studied piano with Sigismund Stojowski, a disciple of Paderewski, and composition with Schönberg. To earn money to support his studies, he accompanied children's ballet classes for a dollar an hour, and played with small dance bands and in speakeasy cabarets. His most lucrative job was as a piano player in the Broadway show *Burlesque*, a role he repeated in the movie version of the same show, called *The Dance of Life*. After 1929, Oscar stayed in Hollywood for the next few years, writing scores for films and about forty popular songs, including the hit "Lady Play Your Mandolin."

In 1929, Brunswick Records asked Oscar to fill in for a pianist who was having difficulty with the piano part for Gershwin's *Rhapsody in Blue*. A few days after the record was made, Gershwin sent for Oscar to tell him that although he liked his interpretation of the piece, he thought his own performance of it was superior. Oscar wasn't offended. Instead, after meeting the handsome, talented Gershwin, he developed such a bad case of hero worship that he began to neglect his own career. He stopped composing and practicing the piano and when he played the piano at all, played only Gershwin's music. Soon he moved in with George and Ira Gershwin, George's lyricist brother, and stayed until Leonore, Ira's wife, ordered him out of the house. In a huff Oscar grabbed his coat and started for the door. Then he stopped. "I'm not leaving," he informed

Leonore. "Why?" she asked. "Because," he confessed sadly, "I have no place to go." He stayed with the Gershwins another two years.

Even though he worshiped George, Oscar could not resist insulting him. Once he asked Gershwin, "George, if you had to do it all over, would you fall in love with yourself again?" George said nothing in reply, but a short while later he retaliated. When he and Oscar were sharing a drawing room on a train, he grabbed the more comfortable lower berth, leaving Oscar the upper. "Upper berth—lower berth. That's the difference between talent and genius," Gershwin pointed out dreamily as the train went rolling on.

Oscar was also a semipermanent houseguest for a while of George S. Kaufman and his wife, Beatrice. He liked to spend long weekends at their farm in Bucks County, Pennsylvania, and after one of his extended visits, Mrs. Kaufman hinted: "The servants always expect a little something. I know you haven't any money, so I tipped them each three dollars and said it was from you." Oscar shouted: "Three dollars? Why didn't you give them five? Now they'll think I'm stingy!"

He never gave up his search for a new set of parents. When his good friends Harpo and Susan Marx adopted a baby boy, he sent them a wire, "Congratulations on your son. If he needs a brother, wire terms."

"I was a penthouse beachcomber," he said when commenting on this period of dependency. "Everything I touched turned to pennies." One evening he spent half the night complaining to Ira Gershwin about his dire financial condition.

"For heaven's sake," Gershwin commented. "How long can you go on like this, Oscar?"

"Another ten years," he replied.

When George Gershwin died suddenly of a brain tumor in 1937, Oscar was devastated. He paid homage to his idol by playing his Concerto in F at a Gershwin Memorial Concert in the Hollywood Bowl. In his pocket was the wristwatch Gershwin had given him. "It became an obsessive ritual; I wouldn't play a concert without it," he said. To ease his distress, he began taking sleeping pills. At first worried that they might become a habit, he asked Dorothy Parker if she took them, too. "Yes," she answered, "in a big bowl with sugar and cream."

Since he had stopped composing and played only the music of Gershwin, he spent a good deal of his time in coffeehouses and restaurants like the old Lindy's on Broadway. Here, amid the raucous bonhomie of songwriters, vaudevillians and wisecracking waiters, he soon acquired a reputation as a sardonic ad-libber and dispenser of insults.

Lindy's in those days was a well-known meeting place for the titans of show business—men who liked to eat and drink heartily and enjoy a belly laugh. It was as famous in its own way as the Algonquin was in its fashion, and sometimes there was stiff competition as to which could produce the most laughs. Sometimes the Lindy's set and the Algonquin set mingled. Although Oscar was never a member of the Round Table, he lunched at the hotel and had friends among the group. In fact, he was more or less granted the supreme accolade when Alexander Woollcott insulted him. "Hmm," Woollcott muttered. "there is absolutely nothing wrong with Oscar Levant that a miracle can't fix."

Woollcott also remarked that arguing with Oscar was "like fighting a man with three hands."

But Oscar preferred Lindy's. Here—in the company of such men as Al Jolson, gangster Arnold Rothstein, and Irving Caesar, the songwriter, he loved to linger and watch the horseplay. Irving Caesar in those days was king of the revels. A famous practical joker, he loved to play jokes on Leo Lindy, the owner. He would telephone Lindy from a phone booth in the restaurant and pretend to be a man from the phone company checking on Lindy's phone, which was next to the cash register. He would ask Lindy to step back a few feet and say "Hello" so he could check the volume. When Lindy obliged, Caesar would then ask him to step back a little farther and speak a little louder. Soon Lindy's yelling of "Hello" could be heard all over the restaurant, and Caesar and his friends would be convulsed with laughter.

Caesar also loved the "Oh Mae" trick. Some unsuspecting patron would be told that a sex-starved married woman lived at a certain address, and all a man had to do to receive her favors was to arrive at her apartment, bearing a strawberry shortcake, knock on her door, and say "Oh Mae."

If the victim believed this tale and decided to act upon it, Caesar and his Broadway buddies would follow him at a discreet distance. They would wait in the shadows, while the poor wretch, carrying his shortcake, knocked on "Mae's" door. Then, when it was flung open, and a man, who was part of the act, appeared in the doorway and yelled, "So you're the man my wife has been seeing when I'm out of town," they would fling down a barrage of light bulbs on the sidewalk outside the apartment. According to Oscar, "the effect was that of bullet shots being fired." Everyone had a good time, except the man with the shortcake, who fled in terror, the light bulbs exploding behind him.

According to Irving Kolodin, Oscar felt like a dislocated person when he moved permanently to California because there was no restaurant like Lindy's in Los Angeles or the Hollywood area, and he felt separated from something that was very much a part of his life. "He enjoyed the casual relationships, going there and seeing who was there, sitting down and having a cup of coffee, and talking," Mr. Kolodin says.

At Lindy's and elsewhere, Oscar never labored to make people laugh. His remarks were impromptu and strictly ad-lib. Groucho Marx and S. J. Perelman regarded him as one of the fastest ad-libbers in the country, rating him with George S. Kaufman and screenwriter Irving Brecher.

Oscar always maintained that he "had no idea of what wit is." He said he had no desire to discuss it. He also believed that it was impossible for a wit to protect his wisecracks. "It doesn't matter who says it first, it's who gets credit for it last that counts."

In 1932, Oscar married Barbara Smith, a dancer. The union lasted a little less than a year. When he heard that Oscar was getting a divorce, Harpo Marx asked him what factors had been responsible.

"Incompatibility," snapped Oscar. "And besides, I had the definite feeling she loathed me."

Soon after the divorce, Barbara remarried movie theater chain tycoon Arthur Loew. On her wedding night, at 2:00 A.M., Oscar called her at her Great Neck estate to inquire: "What's playing at the Loew's State and what time does the feature go on?"

In 1938, Oscar's life changed completely. He was strolling down Fifth Avenue when a young radio producer, Dan Golenpaul, stopped him and offered him a chance to appear on a new radio program, "Information Please." Literary critic Clifton Fadiman was the moderator, and Franklin P. Adams and sportswriter John Kieran were regular members of the panel who attempted to answer questions on sports, literature, music, and current events.

Oscar was the youngest panelist and was known as "l'enfant terrible." Members of the listening audience soon discovered that his brand of wit was unique—no one before him on radio had ever dared to be as sneering, sardonic and frank. Once the panel was asked to name some everyday household expressions. Kieran and F.P.A. answered with, "The front door's ringing" and "Please pass the salt," but Oscar blurted out "Are you going to stay in the bathroom all day?"

Franklin P. Adams wrote an article about the radio show in which he said that when he and Kieran didn't know the answers, they simply kept quiet, but when Oscar didn't know, he was "at his wordiest and sometimes his best under those conditions."

In 1939, Oscar married a petite blonde actress named June Gilmartin. June's stage name was June Gale—she was one of the Gale Quadruplets, two sets of twins who appeared in many Broadway shows. Oscar was smitten with her on their first date and told her, "You have an unawakened face, but your mouth has possibilities." Even though June became his wife, she was never spared his thorny comments. On one of his TV shows, on which she appeared with him, he said, "Because of my attention to other women on the show, my wife told me I ought to get a divorce and settle down." Another time he told the audience that "the main reason I can never fall in love again is that I cannot bear to tell the story of my life all over again." Yet their turbulent marriage endured despite frequent fights and separations. They had three daughters—Marcia, Lorna and Amanda.

Oscar returned to Hollywood in the 1940s and appeared in several more films. Unlike most actors, he was encouraged to write many of his own scenes. The characters he played were very much like himself. He appeared in *Rhythm on the River* with Bing Crosby and Mary Martin (1940), *Humoresque* (1947), *Romance on the High Seas* (1948), *The Barkleys of Broadway* (1949) and *An American in Paris* (1951). He played a left-wing columnist in the screen version of Clare Boothe's comedy, *Kiss the Boys Goodbye* (1941). He also had the role of a Broadway playwright in *The Bandwagon* (1952), a musical film starring Fred Astaire, and played a patient in a sanatorium in *Cobweb* (1955).

In 1945 he played himself in *Rhapsody in Blue*, the story of George Gershwin. For the film he recorded the title piece and the Concerto in F in addition to serving as a consultant on his friend's life.

In Hollywood, Oscar continued to grumble and carp and insult the film colony. His feuds and his wisecracks were always in the gossip columns, and people either hated or loved him on sight.

William S. Targ, his editor at Putnam's, regarded Oscar as "the meanest author in the world." He found Oscar, with his swift mood changes and penchant for late night phone calls, impossible to deal with while he was editing Oscar's last two books, *The Memoirs of an Amnesiac* and *The Unimportance of Being Oscar*. Kenneth Tynan, the drama critic, said his "face awake bears expression of utter disgust most men wear asleep. I am put to mind, uncharitably, of squashed bicycle saddle. Pearl is disease of oyster; Levant is disease of Hollywood." But Tynan liked Oscar and found his eccentricities fascinating. As did Dorothy Parker, who said that "he has no meanness, and it is doubtful if he ever for a moment considered murder." Harpo Marx, too, saw something deeper and more touching in Oscar's perpetual need to hurt.

"The rarest gift Oscar had to offer," Harpo wrote, "was not his virtuosity, but something very few people were fortunate enough to receive—his smile. He didn't give it often, but when he did, it was sunshine in Moscow. His mouth untwisted into a grin, his eyes squinched and twinkled, he ducked his head as sheepishly as a kid caught in some mischief, and in this startling flash of warmth you realized that Oscar for all his sarcasm and sullen cracks, didn't really mean to hurt anybody except himself."

Thanks to the films he played in and the publicity he received, Oscar finally was restored to a career he had always longed for. Suddenly he was much in demand as a concert pianist—particularly playing Gershwin. In fact his annual Gershwin concert at New York's Lewisohn Stadium became an important musical event, and was always a sell-out. Not merely the music lovers but the gangsters and bookies he had cultivated at Lindy's showed up en masse. Even mobster Frank Costello was reportedly crazy about Oscar's piano playing. Levant's "Program of Piano Music with Comments" was also tremendously popular, particularly with college students who flocked by the thousands to gyms and field houses to listen to him play and tell anecdotes about Bach, Paderewski and Gershwin. In the 1940s, more than one hundred of Oscar's recordings of classical piano works by such composers as Khachaturian, Debussy and Beethoven were on the market. He performed with Arturo Toscanini, Eugene Ormandy, Pierre Monteux, Dimitri Mitropoulos and almost every other important conductor in the United States.

When he performed with Toscanini, the volatile maestro disagreed with him over the interpretation of a few passages in Gershwin's Concerto in F. "But Mr. Gershwin wanted it that way," countered Oscar. "That-a poor boy," replied Toscanini. "He was a-sick."

At his concerts Oscar insisted that the audience get there on time. He was in the middle of a piano recital when a woman came late, sweeping down the aisle, and distracting the audience. "I stopped my performance of a Poulenc piece and began choreographing her walk by playing in time with her steps. She hesitated and slowed down—I slowed down. She stopped—I stopped. She hurried—I hurried. By the time she reached her seat, the audience was in hysterics and the matron in a state of wild confusion."

In 1952, exhausted by the pressures of a particularly demanding concert tour, Oscar had a run-in with James C. Petrillo, head of the American Federation of Musicians, and suffered a heart attack. Though only partially recovered, he made the film *The Bandwagon*, and then tried to resume his tour. Overworked and overwrought, he was forced to cancel five scheduled concerts in Canada. Petrillo suspended him from the union, but later agreed to drop the charges if Levant would appear before him and promise to be a good boy in the future. Forsaking his frown and his indolent slouch, Oscar appeared before him and dutifully apologized. The union boss forgave him, but, for Oscar, nothing was quite the same again.

Deeply humiliated and depressed, he sought solace in pills, which deepened his melancholy, and made it more difficult for him to keep his concert engagements and maintain a schedule of work. By the time he died of heart disease in 1972 at the age of sixty-five, he had been treated for drug addiction in several sanatoriums. Typically, he wisecracked even about his drug dependency. "I was voted Pill of the Year by the Pharmaceutical Society," he said. The remark probably didn't seem funny to his daughters or his wife June. Often she had to lock him in his bedroom to keep him from phoning a local quack who was willing to give him pentobarbital injections.

In the late 50s and 60s, he was sometimes a guest on the late-night talk shows, particularly those of Jack Paar and Steve Allen. In gloomy self-absorption, he would ruminate about his own hypochondria, addictions, mental breakdowns and shock treatments. Again and again he would refer to the heart attack he had suffered. On one show he held his hand over his heart and told the audience, "If I didn't hold it, my heart would fall out," a remark which led someone to comment, "At times Oscar resents that anyone else ever had a heart attack."

Even these appearances became too much for him in time, and he preferred to stay at home, "contriving new means of sleeping all day." People who visited him were importuned to bring sleeping pills. "I wake up and the feeling of terror is so knife-edged," he wrote in *The Memoirs of an Amnesiac*. "Just the idea of waking up and facing a day of inertia and fear makes me long for a return to the unconscious. That's one reason why I address sleep with such great reverence; I can escape fear and melancholia. I see sadness everywhere."

Those few friends he saw were shocked by the drastic change in his appearance. He looked like a skeleton. According to Irving Kolodin, "There followed . . . further depressions, more drugs and a pattern of decline impossible for one who saw it to recapitulate. By this time he was living in the house in Beverly Hills where he died. Oscar was dying, gradually but unmistakably, for years before August 14, 1972. Whenever I went to Los Angeles, I would pay him a visit. Once I came at 10 P.M. As I rose to go an hour and a half later, he exclaimed angrily, "You call that a visit!" I always went with trepidation, not knowing quite what to expect. I always left with an awareness that his mind—however disserved by memory lapses and sheer frustration at his lessened physical capacity to articulate—retained its sharp edge, its trenchant wit."

Oscar died on North Roxbury Drive in Beverly Hills, California, a few blocks away from the house where George Gershwin had lived during the most creative period of his life. On the day of his death he practiced the piano as usual.

6

W.C. Fields

Peck's Bad Boy

"I'd rather be dead in Los Angeles than alive in Philadelphia."

W. C. FIELDS became a homeless waif at the age of eleven, and from then on had to live by his wits alone. He slept on park benches and billiard tables, stole free lunches from corner saloons and filched cash from the tills of small Philadelphia shopkeepers. When he grew older and became famous, he never really settled down, remaining a vagabond at heart, doing exactly as he pleased. Fields was a man who cared nothing for conventional behavior. He flouted respectability and poked fun at law and order. All his humor was a kind of endless scoffing and spoofing, an impish defiance of sober society and civilized ways. Fields drank quarts of whiskey a day. He fought with his wife and mistresses, his neighbors, and the people who employed him in movies and on radio shows. Who but Fields would confound the country's banking system by taking out hundreds of bank accounts, most of them under weird pseudonyms? And who but Fields would dare kick his baby co-star in the rear end?

A large man with a nasal drawl, a bulbous nose the color of a raspberry, and an air of fradulent dignity, Fields favored florid speech in ordinary conversation. Referring to an insurance doctor who examined him and refused to give him a policy, he said, "That nefarious quack claimed he found urine in my whiskey."

Fields was a mass of prejudices. He hated lawyers, considering them "knaves and thieves." "The only thing a lawyer wouldn't question is the legitimacy of his own mother." Doctors were "dastardly fee-splitters. When doctors and undertakers meet, they always wink at each other." He mistrusted bankers more, and to outwit them opened more than seven hundred bank accounts all over the world. A few of these accounts were opened under his own name, but most were under pseudonyms—Dr. Otis Guelpe, Larson E. Whipsnade, Ellsworth Boynton and Chester Snavely. Fields maintained that his unorthodox banking methods prevented the Internal Revenue Service from knowing precisely how much money he had. "Uncle Whiskers will strike down even a child and take away its marbles," he said. One year when making out his income tax he tried to deduct his liquor bill, saying he drank alcohol for medicinal purposes. (He didn't get away with it.)

When people asked Fields how he liked children, he usually replied in his wheezy twang, "Parboiled or fried." Or else he would say, "Children should neither be seen nor heard from—ever again."

Fields's vendetta against Baby Leroy, the chubby blue-eyed infant who co-starred with him in several films, was heavily publicized, and many people thought the comedian was merely capitalizing on his reputation as a child hater for comic effect. His friends insisted, however, that the feud was real and that the baby aroused Fields's genuine animosity. They said that he was convinced Baby Leroy was trying to steal scenes from him and had various secret ways of taking revenge. Once he allegedly spiked the baby's orange juice with gin and gloated when Baby Leroy had trouble waking up. "Walk him around, walk him around!" Fields reportedly advised. As Baby Leroy was wheeled home in a state of stupefaction, Fields is said to have shouted, "That kid's no trouper!"

When Baby Leroy and Fields were filming an eating scene in a boardinghouse dining room in *The Old-Fashioned Way*, the infant actor, obeying the script, dropped Fields's watch into the molasses, spilled some soup in his lap, and hit him in the face with a spoonful of ice cream. Following this sequence, Fields had a scene where he was alone with the child, who was creeping along on the carpet. Smiling sweetly, Fields drew back his foot and kicked his tormentor about six feet. In real life, Fields's conscience bothered him, and the next day he appeared at the studio with presents for Baby Leroy. "One of the gifts was a bowie knife," he later joked to a friend.

Years later Baby Leroy, then a grown man working as a lifeguard, said that the orange juice episode was just a publicity gag and insisted that Fields had always been kind to him. Every Christmas Fields sent him and his mother a telegram, and when he heard that Baby Leroy was washed up at the age of three, he had a special part for the tot written into one of his films.

Fields showed no compassion for Edgar Bergen's wooden dummy, Charlie McCarthy. On the air Charlie called Fields "a two-legged martini" and added "You weren't born. You were squeezed out of a bar rag." Fields's answer to this was, "One more crack out of you, and I'll nail runners on your stomach and use you for a sled." On other occasions, he called the dummy "a blockhead, a flophouse for termites," and threatened to slash him into venetian blinds.

As a homeless child who had lived by his wits, Fields had often been attacked by dogs and bitten severely. All his life he was afraid of dogs, and dogs seemed to dislike him. In his profile of Fields in *The New Yorker*, Alva Johnston offers an explanation of this phenomenon. "Fields can give the impression to men that he is a highly respectable fellow," Johnston said, "but he cannot give that impression to dogs. Once a tramp always a tramp, as far as dogs are concerned."

Dogs continued to gang up on Fields throughout his life, even though he tried hard to appease them. According to his biographer Robert Lewis Taylor, Fields was staying at a sanitarium when he read a newspaper story about a dog that had been jailed for drunkenness. The canine lived in a bar, and some regular customers thought it funny to get the dog drunk every night. One evening, when the dog was particularly glassy-eyed, a customer called a policeman, who arrested the dog for drunkenness. After he read the story, Fields called the saloon and told the owner, "Bring the beast to the sanitarium. I want to enroll the misguided creature in Alcoholics Anonymous." When the dog and its owner appeared, Fields, after downing a couple of drinks, gave the dog a stern lecture on the evils of drinking. Afterward he felt disturbed about the dog's miserable life and persuaded the owner to give it to some friends who lived in the country.

Fields's drinking was prodigious. He stocked his house with hundreds of cases of beer and placed quart jars of martinis in strategic spots. Martinis were his favorite drink, and he would start the day with two or three. At lunch, he would drink a few more martinis and a couple of glasses of beer. If he were shooting a movie, he would bring an enormous cocktail shaker of martinis to the set every morning. In the afternoon he would sometimes play golf and would hide a dozen miniatures of gin in his golf bag, explaining that he always kept "a supply of stimulant handy in case I see a snake—which I also keep handy." When he played tennis, it was said that he would grip the racket in one hand and a martini in the other. Rarely did he spill a drop. In Hollywood for a time he was said to have drunk two quarts of whiskey a day. Once, on the air, his straight man asked, "Mr. Fields, what would your father have said if he knew that you drank two quarts of whiskey a day?" "He would have said I was a sissy," Fields replied.

Anecdotes about Fields and alcohol are endless. Once a bartender served him a drink and asked, "Would you like a slice of lemon peel in it?" Fields answered, "If I wanted lemonade, I would ask for it."

To Fields also is attributed the quip, "The dear lady drove me to drink. It's the only thing I'm grateful to her for."

On the set he liked to tell people that his large cocktail shaker contained pineapple juice. One day, when he left the set for a few minutes, some pranksters found the shaker and poured in a generous amount of real pineapple juice. When Fields returned, he poured himself a drink, and then roared, "Somebody's been putting pineapple juice in my pineapple juice!"

One day a young man knocked on the door of Fields's California home and claimed that he was his long-lost son. The comedian was skeptical, but invited him in. "Would you like a drink?" he asked the young man. "No sir, but I'll take a glass of water," the young man replied. "Get out of here," yelled Fields. "You're an obvious imposter!"

Fields had an enormous appetite for liquor, but drinking never seemed to impair his wit or his skill as a juggler. "I have a system," he told a friend, "I know I've had enough when my knees bend backward." Mack Sennett believed that Fields's "timing was better when he was drinking . . . He was sure, sharp, positive." Fields could juggle three cigar boxes after drinking a quart of Irish whiskey. He was also able to drive a car under the influence without getting picked up by the cops. According to Alva Johnston, one snowy night, after drinking a good deal of Irish whiskey, he and a friend started home from Long Island at four in the morning. The next thing they knew, they were in a warm, sunny climate. They had driven all the way to Ocala, Florida, without knowing where they were going or stopping for food or sleep—or hitting a single car.

Although Fields drank constantly, he hated the company of drunks. Any visitor who became intoxicated was never invited back. "Gives drinking a bad name" was how he described a sot.

Fields was born William Claude Dukenfield on January 29, 1880, in Germantown, a suburb of Philadelphia. In later years he liked to invent colorful stories about his background to torment curious reporters and told one paper that his mother and father suffered from leprosy, another that his grandfather made imitation tortoise-shell combs and had been shipwrecked on the shores of America, and another that he came from a long line of actors. "I've got the theater in my blood," he boasted.

Actually Fields's father was a street peddler who eked out a meager living selling fresh fruits and vegetables. He would walk the streets of Germantown with a horse and wagon, calling his wares in a hoarse, whining voice. At a very early age, Fields was forced to accompany his father on his route. Bored, he began to mimic his father's nasal drawl, calling out fruits and vegetables with names strange to Germantown. "Rutabagas! Calabashes! Pomegranates!" When the neighborhood women asked the price of these wonderful fruits and vegetables, Mr. Dukenfield would have to explain that his son was afflicted with an overactive imagination; then, as soon as they left the neighborhood, he would whack the boy for his impudence.

Fields said that his two comic trademarks—his hypocritical heartiness and two-faced nature—were inspired by his mother. According to him, Mrs. Dukenfield would stay in bed till noon, "besotted with gin." At twelve she would get dressed and stand out on the front porch, mopping her brow and saying with a sigh that she had been cooking and doing housework all morning. As her acquaintances passed the house, she would smile at them and murmur some pleasantry, immediately saying something nasty about them as soon as they were out of earshot.

Mr. Dukenfield was a firm believer in discipline and clouted his son regularly. One day, when he was nine, Fields sneaked into a local vaudeville show. A juggling act was going on and he watched it, fascinated. With lemons and oranges pilfered from his father's wagon, he started practicing the art of juggling. "By the time I could keep two objects going in the air simultaneously, I'd ruined forty dollars' worth of fruit," he once recounted.

When his father caught him, he beat him unmercifully. One afternoon Fields carelessly left a rake in the yard, and when Mr. Dukenfield stepped on it, the handle flew up and banged his shin. Seeing Fields smirking at him from a doorway nearby, Mr. Dukenfield picked up the rake and bashed it over the boy's head. In the "Peck's Bad Boy" tradition, Fields evened up accounts with his father the following day by hiding on a ledge above the stable door. When his father entered the stable, he dropped a heavy wooden crate on him. Then he left home, never to return. He was eleven years old.

He began to live like a beggar. He slept in alleys, in caves, in a smithy, on billiard tables and occasionally in Philadelphia jails. He stole milk from milkmen's wagons and free lunches from saloons. He ran errands, learned to mark cards and hawked newspapers on street corners. Strange names fascinated him, and he would stand at busy intersections selling newspapers and shouting such fictitious headlines as "Bronislaw Gimp Acquires License for Two-year-old Sheep Dog!" or "Amos Stump Discovered Living in Eagle's Nest!" If a buyer complained that there were no such stories in the newspaper, Fields would tell him that due to a printer's error, they had been omitted from his particular copy.

Because of constant colds caused by exposure to the weather, his voice eventually hoarsened to a permanent rasp. It became, as someone described it, "the voice of a Caruso with a hangover." As a result of frequent fights, his nose became bulbous and swollen with scar tissue.

Fields was not entranced by his hometown, Philadelphia. The only nice thing he ever said about it was that it was "a great town for breweries." "Philadelphia was a gay, lighthearted town," he sneered. "Anyone found smiling after the curfew rang was liable to be arrested. If a woman dropped her glove on the street, she might be hauled before a judge for stripteasing."

When Fields was fourteen, he saw the Burns brothers, a juggling team, and began practicing for almost sixteen hours a day. After two years, he was employed as a five-dollar-a-week juggler at a summer park in Norristown, Pennsylvania. Following this stint, he was engaged as a juggler and "drowner" at Fortescue's Pier in Atlantic City. When business was brisk on the pier, Fields performed as a juggler. When it slackened, he "drowned." Putting on his bathing suit, he would wade out until the water covered his neck and start yelling for help. Rescued by lifeguards, he would be carried to Fortescue's Pier and rolled over a barrel. Barkers milled through the excited onlookers, urging them to calm their nerves with a little refreshment of beer and sandwiches. Business was often so poor that Fields was forced to "drown" three or four times a day.

When the summer was over, he joined a road company which presented small vaudeville acts. The actors were seldom paid, and most of them quit the show, forcing Fields to play several parts in the same sketch. His salary was eighteen dollars a week, but Fields never received it: One night the manager ran off with the profits.

Through all his professional ups and downs, Fields kept practicing his juggling. Finally, he was booked as a juggler into the best vaudeville houses. He spent a large part of his early career in Europe, South Africa and the South Seas, perfecting his skill to the point where he could balance twenty-five cigar boxes on end with a rubber ball on top.

Now known as "The Tramp Juggler," Fields was signed for the Ziegfeld Follies of 1915. One of his co-stars was a rival comedian, Ed Wynn. During a performance, Fields discovered that Wynn had sneaked under a billiard table on which Fields was wielding a warped cue. Wynn was trying to steal the scene by making funny faces at the audience. Fields thereupon whacked Wynn with the bent cue, knocking him senseless, and continued his game. After the show Fields reportedly told Wynn, who had just revived, that since the audience responded enthusiastically to the whacking, they might incorporate it in the act. Wynn refused the offer.

Fields was a featured performer in every edition of the Ziegfeld Follies through 1921. In the musical *Poppy*, produced in 1923, he played the role of Eustace McGargle, an unctuous charlatan, and established a comic persona which was to distinguish him for the rest of his life.

In one of the scenes in *Poppy*, Fields told his foster daughter his philosophy of life: "My child, a few words of advice. Never give a sucker an even break." The line soon became his catch phrase. Whether he invented it or not is a matter of conjecture. Some authorities credit it to his friend, Wilson Mizner.

Poppy was a hit and after its run ended, Fields made a number of successful pictures, including *The Bank Dick, My Little Chickadee* and *David Copperfield*, in which he gave a highly praised performance in the role of Mr. Micawber. He insisted on writing his own scripts, dashing off a synopsis on the back of an old grocery bill and then selling his treatment to the studio for $25,000. Since it was written into his contract that he had story approval, he would tell the studio that the script was unsatisfactory and then write another for an additional $25,000. Using this method, he was, in one instance, able to make $85,000 on a single screenplay. After he had approved the script, he would then throw it aside and ad-lib most of his dialogue.

Many of his scripts were written under bizarre noms de plume. Otis Criblecoblis, Mahatma Kane Jeeves and Charles Bogle were only a few of the names he put down as authors of his work. Even when a script was completed, he was always adding impromptu remarks. His cure for insomnia was to "get plenty of sleep" and his reason for refusing to take a Bromo Seltzer was that he "couldn't stand the noise." Once, a beautiful girl who was part of his juggling act knocked down a backdrop with a row of houses painted on it. "They don't make houses like they used to," Fields cracked. Another time, when he was alone on stage, marking cards in preparation for a poker game, a stagehand knocked over some trunks in the wings. The theater resounded with a thunderous clamor. Fields stopped marking cards and looked at the audience. "Mice," he confided.

Fields, who mistrusted the writers assigned to him, said that his dialogue was mostly his own invention. "If I did remember my lines, it would be bad for me," he would say. On another occasion, he said the only lines he followed were those of Charles Dickens. Pronouncements like these gave his writers bad dreams.

Most of his fellow actors did not appreciate his ad-libbing either. Mae West was reportedly furious when he departed from the script of *My Little Chickadee* and called her "my little brood mare." A teetotaler, Mae had stipulated that she would make the film only if Fields promised to abstain from alcohol for the duration of the shooting. Staff members were assigned to watch him and prevent any tippling between takes. Fields, of course, outwitted them: He sneaked bottles onto the set swathed in napkins or wrapped up in a parcel. One day he forgot himself and blurted out, "Someone has stolen the cork out of my lunch!" Mae West said that the only thing she and Fields ever had in common was a mutual distaste for a movie called *The Jayhawkers*. They were supposed to star in it but hated it so much that they finally persuaded the studio to throw out the script and film *My Little Chickadee*, a tale they made up as they went along.

As co-stars, Fields and West were constantly competing for laughs. They had a fight about who should get top billing in *My Little Chickadee*. "If you weren't such a ham," said Miss West to Mr. Fields, "you'd admit that never in history has a gentleman been billed ahead of a lady."

"Oh yehss?" retorted her co-star. "How about Adam and Eve?"

Fields usually behaved in a truculent manner toward most Hollywood producers. "His main purpose seemed to be to break as many rules as possible and cause the maximum amount of trouble for everybody," said a studio executive.

When he became a star, Fields demanded and received autonomy in the preparation, direction and production of his films. Perhaps as a result of his vagabond life as a child, he was an arch-antiestablishmentarian, bent on bucking the Hollywood system with all the ingenuity at his command. "Hollywood is the gold cap on a tooth that should have been pulled out years ago," he said.

Gregory La Cava, a director who worked with Fields, believed that the comedian's personal and professional life was dedicated to getting back at society for the deprivations of his childhood. "Nearly everything Bill tried to get into his movies was something that lashed out at the world," he told Robert Lewis Taylor. "The peculiar thing is that although he thought he was being pretty mean, there wasn't any real sting in it. It was only funny. Bill never really wanted to hurt anybody."

Fields's personal life was as complex as his attitude toward his films. Publicly he liked to pretend that he was an old reprobate. Of marriage, he said, "I believe in tying the marriage knot as long as it's around the woman's neck." He also said that a man should "marry an outdoors woman. Then if you throw her out into the yard for the night, she can still survive."

Once when he and a friend were discussing women, the friend asked, "Tell me, Bill. Do you believe in clubs for women?"

"Yehss," was the reply. "If every other form of persuasion fails."

Privately, Fields was rather soft-hearted toward women, however. He hated dirty jokes and frowned when another man told them in front of a woman. If a woman was introduced to him, he always stood up. This instinctive habit got him into trouble one day when his business manager Bill Grady brought a female friend up to his study. It was a warm day, and Fields was sitting stark naked behind his desk. When they burst in, Fields rose. The lady hastily departed.

Fields was married once. His wife was Harriet Hughes, a musical comedy dancer, whom he married at the turn of the century. Her father was a wholesale grocer. Later, when the couple began to have marital difficulties, Fields remarked that for a good part of his life he seemed to have been pursued by vegetables.

At first Harriet and Fields were relatively happy. They lived in New York, and life was serene and domestic. Fields was young and handsome, with luxuriant light-colored hair parted in the middle, and he liked to stay at home at night reading his favorite authors—Swift, Dickens and Mark Twain. During this period he had a rapprochement with his long-estranged family. He invited his mother to his home in New York and gave her tickets to *Poppy* in which he was starring. He even took Mr. Dukenfield on a trip to Europe because his father had always wanted to visit England. It was on this trip to Europe that Harriet became pregnant. A son was born, who was named W. C. Fields, Jr. (he later preferred to call himself Claude). Fields's son grew up to be a staid, respectable lawyer who shunned publicity and alcohol. He died in Hollywood in 1971.

A few years after Claude's birth, Harriet and Fields were separated. Religion was said to have been an important factor in their parting. Harriet was a devout Catholic, while Fields was of the opinion that any minister should be unfrocked immediately and forcefully prevented from imparting his notions to the young. It was also said that Fields's habit of juggling amidst Harriet's cherished bric-a-brac was another source of friction.

Fields had an illegitimate son by Bessie Poole, a Ziegfeld girl. He and Miss Poole lived together in New York for seven years, and after their relationship dissolved, Fields sent her weekly payments for the boy's support. Several years after their breakup, Miss Poole died after her nose was fractured in a nightclub brawl.

In his later years, Fields's constant companion was Carlotta Monti, a pretty young brunette starlet of Italian-Mexican-Spanish descent. She remained with him until the end of his life. Their relationship was a happy one, although not without its tribulations. Carlotta sang professionally, and Fields hated singing because he associated it with his father who used to sing religious and sentimental songs when under the influence of drink. His hatred was so violent that if anyone started singing in his presence, he would leave the room immediately. Carlotta learned to retaliate. If she and Fields had a quarrel, she would lock herself in the bathroom and start singing at the top of her lungs. Like a man gone beserk, Fields would pound on the bathroom door with his cane and in a hoarse bellow threaten to set the house on fire if she didn't stop.

As he grew older, Fields's innumerable eccentricities became more pronounced. He hated birds, for example, and sold one of his homes because it had a small lake which attracted swans and ducks. He said they liked to chase him around the property, hissing and quacking at him. In retaliation, he would often drive a golf ball in a bird's direction, whereupon the bird would chase him around the grounds. "These miscreant fowl break all the rules of civilized warfare," he complained.

His favorite house was on De Mille Drive, a rented Spanish mansion which he allowed to deteriorate because he refused to spend money on repairing a house which someone else owned. "All landlords should be grilled en brochette," he said. As soon as he moved into the mansion, Fields installed a pool table in the drawing room and a ping-pong table in the living room. In the dining room he had a barber's chair, complete with towels and aprons. One of the few joys of his youth was getting a haircut (the ritual made him forget he was poor) and as he grew older and was increasingly troubled by insomnia, he would stretch out in his barber's chair, with the aprons and towels wrapped around him, and at last feel relaxed enough to fall asleep. At other times he was able to get to sleep only by stretching out on the pool table. "A pool table was one of my early beds," he told Carlotta, "and all of us unconsciously revert to our childhood." Sometimes when his insomnia was particularly bad, he could fall asleep only under a beach umbrella on which a garden hose sprinkled imitation rain. According to a friend, "he felt that somehow a moratorium was declared on all his troubles when it was raining."

Although occasionally capable of brief fits of generosity, Fields was miserly with his money. A millionaire, he refused to give Carlotta the funds to pay for a destitute cousin's medical bills. She sold her furniture to pay for them. To save money on telegrams, he was in the habit of running the message together so that it counted as one word: "Wouldbedelightedtoreceiveyourcheck." On telegrams, he never signed his real name but used the pseudonym "Ampico J. Steinway." If the clerk in the telegraph office noted that Ampico J. Steinway had the same address as W. C. Fields, he would say grandly, "He's my butler," and then press a nickel tip into the clerk's hand.

Fields had a running feud with funeral directors, whom he hated because he felt they overcharged for their services. He enjoyed asking funeral directors such questions as "Would a large empty radio cabinet be acceptable for a child's casket?" and "How do I know you're not going to dig up the casket after my funeral and resell it?"

He never trusted any of his servants and locked all the closets where his liquor was stored. When he first met Carlotta, he tested her honesty by planting large sums of money around the house to see if they would disappear.

He was constantly afraid of being burglarized and installed an elaborate intercom system throughout the mansion, concealing loudspeakers everywhere, even beneath a wooden woodpecker which served as a front door knocker.

The master microphone for the system was located in his office. If he was awakened by an unusual sound during the night, he would grab the microphone and snarl, "Don't make a move, I've got you covered," and then go back to bed. Sometimes he spent a good part of the day peering out the windows through binoculars. When people asked him what he was looking for, he said he was searching for "marauding bands of pedestrians."

Deanna Durbin, the teenage soprano who had a voice like a mature woman's, lived next door. She starred in many successful movies, including *One Hundred Men and a Girl* with conductor Leopold Stokowski before she abandoned her career in 1948. Whenever Miss Durbin started practicing her scales, Fields would fling open a window and shout, "Go buy yourself an electric chair!" According to Carlotta, he blamed every dying bush or dead bird on his property on Deanna Durbin. "Her voice is destroying all the flora and fauna in the community. Call the Audubon Society. Call some botany club. If there isn't any, organize one. The woman is a dangerous menace."

Several years before his death, a doctor had told Fields, "Unless you stop drinking, you won't live another six months." "Why, that's exactly what a doctor in Berlin told me twenty-five years ago," Fields replied. "He must have been right!" But finally, in his sixties, with his liver and kidneys irretrievably damaged, drinking was no longer a subject for jest. Fields spent his last years in and out of Las Encinas, an expensive California sanitorium. He was plagued by bouts of delirium and suffered so badly from arthritis that he could not longer use his hands for juggling. His insomnia intensified. Wildly restless at night, he often tumbled out of bed and finally bought an oversized antique cradle and slept in it instead of a bed. Toward the end of his life, a friend asked, "If you had your life to do over, what would you like to change?" Fields paused for a moment before replying. "I'd like to see how I would have made out without liquor," he said.

All during his life Fields had always referred to death as "the fellow in the bright nightgown." Now, he began talking about the fellow in the bright nightgown who would soon pay him a visit. He died in 1946 on Christmas, a day he had always hated because his father had once stolen all the money he had saved as a little boy to buy his mother a present. As he lay dying, he kept quoting long passages from *David Copperfield*. Shortly before noon, he said to Carlotta, "Grab everything and run. The vultures are coming . . . Goddam the whole friggin' world and everyone in it but you, Carlotta." A moment later he died. He was sixty-six years old.

Following his death, his heirs bickered over his estate and the disposition of his body. A non-believer, Fields had stipulated that he wanted no funeral service of any sort and requested that his body be immediately cremated. Harriet Fields, from whom he had been separated for more than thirty years, came forward, however, and insisted on a large public funeral. It was followed by a private Catholic ceremony, which she also instigated. Carlotta, who was an ardent believer in the supernatural, then organized a third funeral, based on spiritualism.

The comedian had left his son Claude and Harriet Fields each $10,000. Carlotta was given $25 weekly for the rest of her life. The bulk of his estate, approximately $800,000 in cash, was earmarked for the establishment of the "W. C. Fields College for Orphan Boys and Girls, Where No Religion of Any Sort is to be Preached." But Harriet Fields contested the will, claiming half the $800,000 as automatically hers under California property law, and after seven years of legal wrangles, eventually won more than half the estate. Fields's orphanage was never built.

He was buried in Forest Lawn, an elaborate Hollywood cemetery which had often been the subject of his jokes. Many people believe that his celebrated remark, "On the whole, I'd rather be in Philadelphia," is engraved on his tombstone, but the inscription reads simply. "W. C. Fields: 1880–1946."

7

Texas Guinan

"Hello, Sucker!"

"Marriage is all right, but I think it's carrying love a little bit too far."

DURING THE 1920s, bored millionaires in search of diversion, gawking out-of-towners, and gangsters with their molls liked to squeeze into tiny smoke-filled rooms to be heckled and amused by a breezy middle-aged blonde who called herself Texas. Perched atop a grand piano, she hurled wisecracks, insults and primitive jokes at her enchanted audience. On her fleshy fingers sparkled numerous rings set with huge glittering diamonds. Even in that bizarre era of speakeasies, bootleggers and rum runners, Texas Guinan was a phenomenon, a special product of the Prohibition era. She was in a way its essence—with her flamboyance, her zest for life and her raucous irreverence.

A minor vaudeville and silent picture actress who had once lamented that she "was so far back in the chorus they had to take a brick out of the wall to find me," she and some friends went to a party one night at the Beaux Arts Hotel in New York. The gathering was dull, so Texas decided to enliven it by singing a few songs. Her audience was entranced, although not by her singing, which was passable at best. Nor were they captivated by her appearance—her overbleached hair, her prominent teeth, and her figure (buxom bordering on the obese). What delighted the crowd were the impudent comments she fired off between songs. In fact, the hotel manager was so impressed that he immediately offered her a job as mistress of ceremonies at the Beaux Arts. Thus Texas Guinan began her career as one of the 20s' most popular entertainers. She was thirty-eight years old.

Prohibition had been in effect for four years, but in practice, the nation was far from dry. Thousands of speakeasies had sprung up overnight, offering illegal alcohol and after-hours entertainment. Many of these nightspots were backed by gangsters who charged as much as $25 for a bottle of bootleg Scotch and $2 for a pitcher of plain water to go with it. It was not uncommon for four or five people to run up a $1,000 bill for an evening.

One of the best-known New York speakeasy proprietors of the 20s was Larry Fay, a tall, horse-faced racketeer who owned the Club El Fey at 107 West 55th Street. Fay was a unique kind of gangster who had started life driving a cab and soon owned a fleet of taxis so brilliantly painted that a passenger could spot one a mile away. He loved to give fur coats to chorus girls and often paid their funeral expenses.

Larry liked Texas's style and thought she would be a great addition to his newly opened nightspot. There, dressed in a slinky red dress, with pearls and diamonds liberally spattering her voluptuous bosom, she cheerfully greeted customers with the words, "Hello, Sucker!," a phrase coined by her friend Wilson Mizner. The salutation soon grew famous. Then, with one hand gripping a police whistle and the other a wooden noisemaker, she sang mocking verses about the celebrities of the Jazz Age. Her targets included the glamorous evangelist Aimee Semple McPherson, dapper Jimmy Walker, mayor of New York, and handsome blonde Edward, the bachelor Prince of Wales who had visited America and set the hearts of the Long Island debs awhirl. When she wasn't singing, Texas would toss off wisecracks considered crackling in their time: "Hollywood sounds like something for a Christmas decoration, but it's just Western for poison ivy"; "A politician is a fellow who will lay down your life for his country"; and "It's having the same man around the house that ruins matrimony." This volley was followed by seminude dancing performed by different members of her troupe of twelve gorgeous girls. At the end of every number, she would ask the customers to "give the little girl a great big hand," a rallying cry that has remained in the language.

She also spawned the phrase "big butter-and-egg man," to characterize a lavish spender from out of town. The story goes that the original butter-and-egg man was a shy, middle-aged gentleman who was so flattered by Texas's friendliness that he paid the steep cover charge for every guest in the place and pressed fifty-dollar bills on all the entertainers. Overwhelmed by such largesse, Texas asked him what he did, and he said he was in the dairy business. She then introduced him from the floor as "the big butter-and-egg man," a phrase which was soon applied to any man who liked to throw money around.

Texas Guinan was born in 1883 near Waco, Texas. Her Irish immigrant parents christened her Mary Louise Cecilia, three solemn-sounding names which she soon shed, adopting the punchier and raunchier-sounding "Texas" in honor of her native state. Her independence and love of mischief were apparent in her childhood. Once, she ran away from home and was later discovered by her distraught parents asleep in a bed in a display window of the local department store. Adoring luxury, she was wrapped in the store's most expensive sheets and blankets. In school one day, discovering that some of her answers to a test had been wrong, she slipped three mice into her teacher's desk and then, when the startled woman fled from the room, quickly changed the answers to the correct ones.

A conventional existence was bound to be unappealing. Texas soon left home to become a cowgirl in a Wild West show. After a short stint in vaudeville, she tackled Hollywood. The famous western star William S. Hart had just left the Triangle Film Corporation, and its president, Harry Atkin, was so intrigued by Texas's lariat-twirling and riding skills as well as by her ability to do all her stunts herself that he hired her and billed her as "The Female William S. Hart." She made more than two hundred two-reel westerns. "We never changed the plots, only the horses," she said of her silent screen career.

Hollywood and its mores inspired her special brand of wit. She once described movie directors as "going around carrying a chip on their shoulders, which is a true indication of wood—a little higher up." As for lasting relationships in Tinseltown, she dismissed the possibility with a wisecrack: "Marriage in Hollywood starts with a rough draft. There's very little work on the continuity."

Unlike the lean and lanky Mr. Hart, Texas was on the heavy side. She waged a lifelong battle against overweight. "I go up and down the scale so often that if they ever perform an autopsy on me, they'll find me like a strip of bacon—a streak of lean and a streak of fat." Once, when she was on a crash diet, she told a reporter: "I want to get as thin as my first husband's promises."

Unfortunately, for Texas, getting thin meant getting into

trouble. In 1914, after she had successfully shed seventy pounds, she was persuaded by a sharp promoter to lend her name to an anti-fat formula. This concoction, composed of alcohol, white iodine and alum, was called the Texas Guinan Anti-Fat Preparation, and guaranteed the corpulent instant weight loss if it was rubbed into their excess flesh. Texas had few qualms about endorsing the product. Her good friend, the actress Lillian Russell, had used a similar preparation and achieved results—it was said.

The product, offered by mail, made its inventors a fortune. Soon they decided to cut corners, decreasing the amount of alcohol and increasing the alum. In no time the nation's fatties were complaining of a new problem, a frightful rash accompanied by a tormenting itch on the spots where they had applied the solution. Texas was arrested, charged with defrauding innocent people through the mails. While she was awaiting trial, the promoter of the product fled the state.

She was tried for fraud and eventually acquitted. It would not be her only experience with the courts, however. Later, to reporters, she made light of her arrest.

A master of self-promotion, she thrived on publicity, courting it even to the point of inventing false marriages and divorces, and concocting tales of wretched orphans she had rescued from the gutter. She told the press that she had had three husbands, adding that she had been wed "twice in earnest and once in Newark." Her first husband was dead, she said. "If my poor, dear departed husband were alive, he would have made a grand aviator—he was no good on earth." Only after she died was it discovered that she had been married only once, and her ex-husband was very much alive. He was John J. Moynahan, a Boston newspaperman. Her other two marriages to a "drama critic" and a "European millionaire" had been fabricated to make her life seem more colorful.

When Texas met Moynahan in 1904, she was engaged to

another man, but pawned this man's engagement ring so she and John could have a honeymoon. The marriage was not a success. According to Moynahan, Texas loathed domesticity and cared only for her career. After the couple separated, she began drifting from man to man. Many were gangsters on whom she squandered most of her earnings. But she committed herself to no one permanently and perhaps revealed her real feelings about men when she said, "Oh, he was all right as sweethearts go—and he went." Of another admirer, she remarked: "He brought me so many orchids that I looked like a well-kept grave."

Diamonds, particularly huge ones, became an obsession. She liked to wear rings on almost every finger and from four to eight bracelets—a few real, mostly fakes—on either arm. Walking down the street, she so dazzled the eye that a friend once compared her to a traveling pawnshop.

As another eccentricity she began to sign her photographs with her thumbprint instead of her name, pressing her thumb into a little pad of purple ink she carried around with her. "There is more individuality in the thumbprint than in the mere writing of one's name," she said. She also made a kind of fetish of never knowing what time it was—often appearing at people's apartments at six in the morning dressed in evening clothes. And she collected odd animals—Pekingese dogs, canaries, and a parrot who yelled "Hello, Sucker!" and "Go to Hell!" Sometimes she would take her menagerie for rides in her gray Excelsior, an armored car with bulletproof tires that had been built for the King of Belgium and later owned by her friend, Larry Fay, who replaced the machine gun turret in the back with a radio. Texas finally persuaded Fay to sell her the car, and as soon as she got it, attached license plates which read: "Texas 1—and Last."

Although she was by nature sweet-tempered, she could be

Alexander Woollcott as "The Town Crier" on CBS radio. *(R. H. Hoffmann, New York Public Library Picture Collection)*

Robert Benchley at his home in Hollywood in 1937. A whimsical practical joker, he once switched neighbors' sofas by posing as a mover. (*Billy Rose Theatre Collection, The New York Public Library at Lincoln Center, Astor, Lenox and Tilden Foundations*)

George S. Kaufman, in 1916, when he was drama editor of the *New York Tribune*. He had not yet achieved fame as a playwright and lothario. (*Culver Pictures*)

Dorothy Parker with her husband Alan Campbell, whom she called "the wickedest woman in Paris." (*Culver Pictures*)

Oscar Levant at the piano, surrounded by coffee, cigarettes and the sports page. (*Culver Pictures*)

W. C. Fields drinking a bottle of milk on the set of Paramount's *The Big Broadcast of 1938*. The comedian's favorite beverage was far less wholesome. *Above*, The W. C. Fields–Charlie McCarthy feud was bitter and prolonged. Charlie called Fields "a two-legged martini," and Fields retorted, "One more crack out of you, and I'll nail runners on your stomach and use you for a sled." (*Culver Pictures*)

Texas Guinan with feathered friends in her cluttered Greenwich Village apartment. The parrot was trained to yell her famous salutation, "Hello, Sucker!" (*Billy Rose Theatre Collection, The New York Public Library at Lincoln Center, Astor, Lenox and Tilden Foundations*)

Texas Guinan draws a crowd in New York City as she steps from her armored limousine. After her death in 1933, it was sold at auction for $80. (*Billy Rose Theatre Collection, The New York Public Library at Lincoln Center, Astor, Lenox and Tilden Foundations*)

Wilson Mizner, playwright, gambler and con man, earned notoriety in the 20s for his brilliant remarks and amazing life. He and his brother Addison were fellow wits whose casual wisecracks were often credited to others. They died within weeks of each other. (*Culver Pictures*)

Marie Dressler, actor Richard Barthelmess and Addison Mizner (center) admire The Cloister in Boca Raton, Florida, one of Mizner's fantastic architectural masterpieces. Addison was as unique a wit as he was an architect. He omitted staircases from his houses and once said that "Isadora Duncan is a bore when drunken." (*Culver Pictures*)

Tallulah Bankhead drinking champagne out of her own shoe at the Ritz Hotel in London in 1951. As she grew older, Tallulah's pranks became increasingly bizarre. (*Wide World Photos*)

Left, Tallulah Bankhead as Cleopatra in Shakespeare's *Antony and Cleopatra.* Although the 1937 production was much ballyhooed, it was a failure. Known for her irreverent remarks, Tallulah was on the receiving end this time. Cracked critic John Mason Brown: "Tallulah Bankhead barged down the Nile last night as Cleopatra—and sank." (*New York Public Library Picture Collection*)

Mrs. Longworth at home on her eighty-fifth birthday. The Chinese tiger scroll in the background was one of the many exotic possessions that filled her home on Dupont Circle in Washington, D.C. (*Wide World Photos*)

Left, "Princess Alice" when she lived at the White House and was the reigning beauty of her day. Even then, she was known for her saucy wit and malicious comments. (*New York Public Library Picture Collection*)

Left, Groucho Marx and Lotta Miles in *I'll Say She Is!*, 1924. In spite of his angelic appearance in this photo, Groucho delighted in needling his female co-stars. (*Billy Rose Theatre Collection, The New York Public Library at Lincoln Center, Astor, Lenox and Tilden Foundations*)

Below, Groucho Marx at home with his younger daughter, Melinda. Groucho once told the headmistress of Melinda's school, "Madam, do you realize that in a few years fifty percent of these children will be getting alimony?" (*Culver Pictures*)

nasty to people she didn't like. Of a celebrated Broadway actress, she remarked: "Her brain is as good as new," and dismissed another with the crack: "She had a heart of gold and teeth to match." She had absolutely no use for men who played around. "A guy who'd cheat on his wife would cheat at cards," she said with high contempt. Hecklers at her club received an instant put-down. "Your behavior is rotten," she said to a man who was making a nuisance of himself. "And that's only a hint."

Her seven-room apartment at 17 West 8th Street in Greenwich Village was described by a friend as "a cross between a Chinese joss house, a Hindu bazaar and a little bit of 'Ye Old Curiosity Shoppe.'" Here she lived with her mother and father, whom she had brought from Texas. The apartment was usually kept dark or else very dimly lit, like an underground grotto. Most of the furniture was draped with Spanish shawls. In the living room were shelves filled with silver, much of it gifts from gangster Al Capone, who had backed one of her clubs in Chicago. A motley collection of cheap cutlery and pewter objects that she had picked up from various hotels she had patronized was also part of the furnishings. The bedroom was small—it was also the darkest room in the apartment. It had no natural light; the windows had been painted black to create the impression of perpetual night. Pictures of Texas and her boyfriends covered the walls. Incense burned day and night, and the whole effect was so unusual that a delivery boy phoning from the apartment to his boss at the grocery store once reported that he was "either in a dope den or a madhouse."

Whether because of or in spite of her eccentricities, many people of the period adored her. Even Edmund Wilson, the novelist and erudite book critic, was captivated. In rhapsodic prose, he described her as "this prodigious woman, with her pearls, her glittering bosom, her abundant beautifully bleached yellow coiffure, her formidable trap of shining white teeth, her broad bare back behind its grating of green velvet, the full-blown peony as big as a cabbage exploding on her broad green thigh."

The Prince of Wales was also an admirer and frequent visitor to her club. Once he was caught in a raid, but the Feds never realized his true identity, thanks to Texas who hustled him off to the kitchen, plunked a chef's hat atop his head and, shoving a skillet into his hand, told him to keep frying eggs until the coast was clear.

At Texas's innumerable clubs, mostly concentrated in the West Forties and Fifties, the atmosphere was rowdy, jam-packed and always intimate. People started drifting in through the canopied entrance at about eleven o'clock, although an occasional customer might arrive as late as five in the morning. Once inside, the patron had to thread his way through a crush of waiters, cigarette girls and couples dancing cheek-to-cheek on the dimly lit postage-stamp dance floor. If he was lucky, he'd find a table and be able to order a drink at a steep price. Then, as the band grew louder, and the impatient guests began to clack wooden noisemakers, Texas, in her clinging red gown, would make a dramatic entrance, with the "gang," a group of girlish beauties, following behind. Holding up her diamond-bedecked hand, she would silence the crowd and begin to sing. Her opening number was guaranteed to bring down the house:

"Let's turn this into a whoopee place and have a lot of fun,
And if we sing about you, why, don't get up and run,
We'll sing about the Broadway folks and anyone you choose,
It'll save you then from buying the *Graphic, Mirror* and the *News.*

Chorus

"Oh it's in the *Graphic* and the *Mirror* and the *News*,
It's funny but no matter which you choose,
Every time I lift my face, or the coppers raid my place,
It's in the *Graphic* and the *Mirror* and the *News*."

After this opening selection, Texas would sing songs about any celebrity who happened to be in the public eye. For example, when Mae West was sentenced to ten days in jail in 1926 for "corrupting the morals of youth and others" with her play *Sex*, Texas sang a verse about Miss West which ran:

"Mae West, my pal, was guilty, she spent ten days in jail.
The day she was convicted, the poor old gal turned pale.
The Judge, they say, fell hard for Mae, with passion which was real.
He said, 'You know, my dear, I'd love to try your sex appeal.'

Chorus

"And they put it in the *Graphic* and the *Mirror* and the *News*."

Then Texas would begin to exchange jokes with her girls and several comedians who were part of her act.

GIRL: "My goodness, Texas, what beautiful jewelry you have!"

TEXAS: "Goodness has nothing to do with it [a line made famous by Mae West]. But, oh girls, I feel wonderful this evening. I feel great—I only weigh 138 pounds."

STRAIGHT MAN: "Stripped?"

TEXAS: "I don't know. The drugstore was too crowded. Isn't he fresh? Now ladies—and whatever you brought with you—I am going to present some of my little girls. This is Esther, she is the baby of the troupe."

COMIC: "She was a baby when Pike's Peak was a pimple."

TEXAS: "Cookie, you are a pain in the neck."

COMIC: "Thanks for moving me up."

Texas's scantily clad girls were an important part of her act and were carefully picked for their talent and pulchritude. They often went on to bigger careers on the Broadway stage or in Hollywood. Among them was Ruby Keeler, who later starred in *42nd Street* with Dick Powell and who became one of the popular musical comedy stars of the era. Ruby, who tap-danced and sang in a lisping baby voice, was a favorite with the male patrons, particularly the gangster Johnny Irish and the jazz singer Al Jolson (whom she eventually married). Some years later, Walter Winchell wrote a film in which Texas played herself. It was called *Broadway Through a Keyhole* and was all about a chorus girl who broke up with a gangster and then married a jazz singer. To some critics, the plot seemed reminiscent of Ruby Keeler's relationship with Irish and her marriage to Jolson. In any case, Jolson resented this invasion of his privacy and slugged Winchell one night at the Hollywood Bowl; in retaliation, the columnist sued him for five million dollars. When Texas heard about the slugging, she shrugged: "Al just wanted to see how somebody else would look on one knee."

Among Texas's male protégés was George Raft, who worked as a tap dancer at her 300 Club, and Rudolph Valentino, who ran the flower concession at her Beaux Arts Café and whom she talked out of becoming a businessman.

Probably the most unique patron ever to visit the club was

Aimee Semple McPherson, the evangelist. In her own way, of course, Mrs. McPherson was every bit as theatrical as Texas. As Texas said: "Aimee and I are the two greatest exhibitionists in the world. We are so much alike we could exchange roles in five minutes. She worked one portion of the public and I worked another, and there proved to be a sufficient number of suckers to go around. She went out for saving souls, and I went out for saving heels."

Aimee, like Texas, was late in achieving fame. Twice married, she left her second husband and, accompanied by her mother and two small children, drove up and down the East Coast, stopping in little towns to pitch a tent and preach the gospel. While speaking in San Diego, she became an overnight sensation when a crippled woman rose from her wheelchair and staggered toward her, cured. Aimee always denied that she was a miracle worker, however. "I am not a healer. Jesus is the healer. I am only the little office girl who opens the door and says 'Come in.' "

In 1923, she founded the Angelus Temple in Los Angeles. On top of this immense structure stood a huge illuminated revolving cross which was visible for fifty miles. Five thousand people could attend her services, which were perked up by Hollywood effects. One of her most colorful spectacles was called "Throw-Out-the-Lifeline." Twelve beautiful girls would cling to a Rock of Ages as a full gale, complete with thunder and lightning, was in progress. Just as the girls seemed about to collapse, Sister Aimee, dressed as an admiral, appeared on stage and ordered a group of female sailors to throw a lifeline to the girls on the rock, while a male chorus dressed in Coast Guard uniforms sang a hymn and combed the artificial waves with searchlights. The girls were rescued, and the American flag waved grandly over all.

On the night Aimee McPherson first appeared at Texas's

club, the first thing she said was, "I am going to lead the singing of some beautiful hymns. There is one little girl here who doesn't know any hymns, and I'm sorry for her." Texas's snappy comeback was, "Sister, I've forgotten more hims than you'll ever know. What's more, I've got all their telephone numbers."

Some years later, Texas, returning the visit, went to the Angelus Temple. For the occasion she wore a picture hat, a fur stole, red high-heeled shoes and most of her diamonds. Stepping out of her limousine, she ascended the church steps and, once inside, immediately prostrated herself at the altar with a moan. Then, as the choir sang "Come to Jesus," she dropped a twenty dollar bill into the collection plate and marched out to the tune of "Praise God from Whom All Blessings Flow." As the cameras clicked, Texas told the swarm of reporters that she wanted to help Aimee spread the gospel. "I'm going to practice nightclub evangelism," she said. "I'm going to save the souls of some of the fools I've made."

At the time, many people believed that her promise was a publicity stunt. Yet her manager and press agent John Stein believed she was serious. As Texas grew older, she began searching for more spiritual values. "I'm going to preach, not religion—but the gospel of happiness," she told a *Los Angeles Examiner* reporter. "I want to bring home the value of tolerance and kill the viciousness of narrow-mindedness. It is something I have thought about for a long time."

Perhaps some of this feeling on her part was inspired by the death of her close friend and longtime companion, Larry Fay. No one knows the nature of their relationship, but Texas seems to have understood all of Larry's foibles, which included dressing like a dandy, painting his fingernails a bright red and taking long automobile rides from Los Angeles to New York in one of his own cabs. He did not seem to mind being hauled off to jail. Larry, who was Public Enemy #3 (John Dillinger was Public Enemy #1), was arrested at least forty-six times but was never convicted of a felony.

Despite making millions, Larry died broke. Shot to death by a drunken doorman at one of his clubs, he was found with three dimes in his pocket. Most of his money had been lost in the stock market crash of 1929, but, according to those who knew Larry well, what ruined him was his self-defeatist attitude. According to a friend, "Larry was probably the greatest failure racketeering has ever known. He was in a position to control the milk, grocery, dry cleaning, laundry and taxi rackets, not to mention the speakeasy field. However, he was either muscled out by someone with a little more nerve or else got tired and quit to try something new."

Texas was shocked by his murder. They had quarreled when she left the Club El Fey to start her own 300 Club on West 54th Street, and El Fey had subsequently failed. Not even the success of his new club, the Rendezvous, and his discovery of a new comedian named Jimmy Durante had soothed Larry's wounded feelings. Just before he died, they became friends again.

When Texas went to the morgue to identify his body, she wept. She paid the mobster's unpaid hotel bill at the St. Moritz, telling friends, "I know he would have done this for me."

In spite of her grief and resolutions about religion, she soon resumed her usual life-style: running her clubs and opening new ones when they were invariably raided by the feds. Although she was never arrested by the two most celebrated Prohibition agents of the period, Isadore Einstein and Moe Smith—quick-change disguise artists—her clubs were constantly being closed by a childhood acquaintance, a Mrs. Mabel Walker Willebrandt. Of Mrs. Willebrandt, an Assistant

United States Attorney General, Texas said: "I knew her when she was a bathing beauty—and she's still all wet." But Texas seems to have taken the raids good-naturedly. Once when a federal agent put his hand on her shoulder and said, "Let's give this little girl a great big handcuff," she asked the band to strike up "The Prisoner's Song" as she was being led away. At the police station, she often invited the dry agents to have a drink with her, a bravado gesture, since Texas never touched a drop. As a symbol of defiance, she began to wear a necklace strung with little gold padlocks, each one engraved with the name of one of her clubs that had been raided and closed.

Although she was arrested and rearrested, Texas never spent a night in jail.

In 1927 she was finally brought to trial for violating the Prohibition laws. Clarence Darrow refused to defend her, believing that she could not win. But Darrow failed to take into account Texas's publicity sense. Discarding the bizarre clothes she habitually wore, she appeared in court dressed in a black velvet suit, carrying a dainty lavender lace handkerchief and a vial of smelling salts. She wisecracked with the judge, treated the Prohibition agents like muddled patrons at her club and was cleared of all charges.

But not even she—with all her resources—could inject life into a dying institution. The heydey of the rowdy nightclub was coming to an end, as people began to prefer the more sophisticated supper clubs that offered smooth music and low-key surroundings. Then suddenly Texas no longer had a club on Broadway—and no one really knew why, although many rumors circulated. Some thought that the night club business was so bad there was no point in trying to stay open. But most people felt it was because she had refused to cut in the notorious gangster Dutch Schultz on a new revue she was rehearsing. When Schultz appeared at the theater and arrogantly demanded the cut, she reportedly threw him out, and in retaliation he made sure that she never performed in New York again.

Texas went off to Paris with her showgirls—and a white horse—but the French would not let her into the country. They gave no specific reason for denying her entry, but rumor ran rampant. Her act was too scandalous; she might bring gangsters into the country; she did not have a labor permit; her night club act would mean loss of revenue for French café owners. Genet of *The New Yorker* was perhaps the most discerning when she wrote: "In general, the French had more trouble with Texas's name than her reputation. She was easier to deport than to pronounce. The Parisian press gave the little girl a great big hand but not where she probably expected it. The French are fascinated by America's night life but only in print. Nor are they starved, their history being what it is, for colorful personalities."

Characteristically, Texas laughed off the rebuff. "I've been thrown out of better places than this," she said. Returning to the States, she capitalized on the experience and started a vaudeville tour with her girls in a review called "Too Hot for Paris." The tour included a stopover at the 1933 Chicago World's Fair.

Too hot for Paris and a bomb at the Fair, Texas decided to move on to Vancouver, British Columbia. There, she was stricken with violent stomach cramps and taken to a nearby hospital, where the doctors diagnosed her condition as colitis. She seemed to be recovering satisfactorily when her large intestine ruptured, and an emergency operation was performed. She never regained consciousness and died on November 5, 1933.

She was forty-nine years old.

The woman who once said "I would rather have a square inch of New York than all the rest of the world" was taken back to Broadway, over which she had reigned for eleven untrammeled years. Not since Valentino's death had Broadway seen such a funeral. Hers was almost as big as his. Thousands of people thronged Campbell's Funeral Parlor at Broadway and 66th Street, stumbling over newsreel and radio cables as they were slowly ushered upstairs to the Gold Room where Texas, lying in a silvered bronze coffin, was being photographed for the newsreels. Her friend Valentino, dead at thirty-one of peritonitis, had lain in the same spot seven years before in a sealed bronze coffin revealing only his face, for it was feared his corpse might be stripped naked by souvenir hunters. In retaliation, his fans had made off with most of the furnishings from the Gold Room.

Texas in death wore the same glittering gown she had worn in her picture, *Broadway Through a Keyhole.* It was of pale gray chiffon smothered with sequins and glass bead embroidery. On her eyelids were the inch-long false lashes she never denied buying from the five-and-ten. Around her neck was a diamond necklace, or what looked like a diamond necklace. And on her wrists were bracelets set with the same sparkling jewels.

But her funeral, like her life, was not without complications. When the authorities learned that her illness had been caused by amoebic dysentery, which she had caught at the World's Fair, they insisted that her coffin be hermetically sealed.

The service in the Campbell chapel was brief. A priest read a short prayer, and then the writer Heywood Broun made a few tearful remarks.

At the Gates of Heaven Cemetery in Valhalla, New York,

pandemonium broke loose. As the priest conducted the service in a receiving vault, a crowd of two thousand souvenir hunters, most of them women, pushed their way into the vault and began ripping off the thousands of flowers on Texas's funeral bouquets. The mob had arrived hours before and managed to overpower the police and state troopers who were standing guard in the cemetery. Women were trampled. Graves were overrun. Inside the receiving vault, women sobbed and screamed when they were unable to push their way up to the coffin. Others scrambled on the roof of the vault and peered in through a skylight at the casket being rapidly despoiled of its orchids and violets, its hundreds of roses.

When the crowd finally departed, the vault was littered with torn ribbons, crushed hats, handbags and petals. On the ground, stripped of their flowers, lay the frames of all the wreaths and sprays.

Alone, in the littered vault, Texas lay in her sealed coffin. Not a single flower was left. Even the arrangement on top of her casket had been destroyed.

Exactly one month after her death, on December 5, the Twenty-first Amendment was ratified. Liquor could now be legally served. Prohibition, which had made her into one of the most bizarre figures in an improbable decade, was over.

8

The Merry Mizners

"Life's a tough proposition, and the first one hundred years are the hardest."

Wilson Mizner

"Many are called, but few get up."

Addison Mizner

WILSON MIZNER was basically a confidence man, although at various times he was a gold rush prospector, a cardsharp, a successful Broadway playwright and Hollywood screenwriter, a medicine man, a boxer, manager of the middleweight champion of the world and a trained bear, a real estate promoter, the proprietor of New York's sleaziest hotel, owner of the Brown Derby and, for a very brief time, husband of the "second richest woman in the world."

In the opinion of many, he was a great wit, a latterday Samuel Johnson. Many of his admirers were theatrical people and writers who jotted down his witticisms and later claimed them as their own. Damon Runyan called Wilson "the greatest man-about-town that any town ever had." Anita Loos called him "the riffraff's Shakespeare" and said "Wilson had the most terrific vocabulary and culture, but he rose above it and kicked culture in the teeth. Listening to the poetry of Shakespeare is the only comparison to Wilson's wit."

In the 20s Wilson Mizner liked to frequent an all-night restaurant called Jack Dunstan's on Sixth Avenue in New York. A tall striking man who often wore a silk top hat and Inverness cape and carried a white-handled cane, he would sit tossing off witticisms till the early hours of the morning. Some of the memorable ones were: "If you copy from one author, it's plagiarism, if you copy from two, it's research." Or: "Be nice to people on your way up because you'll meet them on your way down." Or: "Hollywood is a trip through the sewer in a glass-bottomed boat." Or, of a movie producer who was insufferably pompous: "A demitasse cup would fit over his head like a sunbonnet."

When a judge once asked Wilson if he was trying to show contempt of court, he replied, "No, I'm trying to conceal it." To a friend who congratulated him on a short story he had just written he said, "I wanted to see something of mine in print besides my thumbs." While he was part owner of the Brown Derby restaurant in Hollywood, he was once forced to endure the inanities of a bearded patron, and exclaimed after the man left, "Now I know that hair can grow on anything!" After a burglar, one of his many underworld friends, put the squeeze on him for a loan, Wilson drawled: "Doesn't it get dark anymore?"

Among his miscellaneous quips are: "Treat a whore like a lady and a lady like a whore"; "A good listener is not only popular everywhere, but after a while he knows something"; "Those who welcome death have only tried it from the ears up"; and "The days just prior to marriage are like a snappy introduction to a tedious book." H. L. Mencken was sufficiently impressed by Wilson's statement "I respect faith, but doubt is what gets you an education" to include it in his *New Dictionary of Quotations*.

Wilson was the wit who, on being told that President Calvin Coolidge was dead, asked, "How can they tell?"—a crack often attributed to Dorothy Parker.

He was an accomplished practical joker who would do a lot for a laugh. In the hospital for an appendectomy, he was asked to fill in a form saying where his body should be sent in the event of his death. Without hesitation, he furnished the name and address of a man who loathed him.

After he was admitted to the hospital, a nurse wrote his name, illness, doctor's name, and room number on his chest for identification purposes. "For some reason this extensive identification was not soothing," he later wrote. "It spoke of mix-ups in transit to the slaughterhouse on the top floor. It also breathed of helpless unconsciousness on the part of the tabulated victim. I could see by the glint in my jailer's eye that she had a horrifying answer ready should I inquire about it. So I remained silent, stole her pencil, waited till her back was turned and added this postscript, 'Keep in a cool place till opened.' "

Wilson was a natural-born gambler, and it was said that he would bet on anything. Once he jumped off a ferryboat in San Francisco Bay. When he was picked up, he was floating along staring at his stopwatch and betting with himself on how long it would take before he was rescued. Another time he bet a friend that more people would stare at him on the street than at the friend. He stipulated that neither was to make any bizarre facial movements or grotesque gestures. At the appointed hour, he arrived at New York's 42nd Street with a Great Dane. He and his friend started walking down opposite sides of the street, and by the end of two blocks, almost a thousand people were trailing Wilson. Puzzled, the friend crossed the street and followed Wilson and the dog, which on closer inspection proved a rare animal indeed: Its genitals were painted a bright gold!

Wilson had a brother named Addison, and any study of Wilson must take into account the importance of Addison in his life. The two brothers were close. They were both immensely tall men, well over six feet, and Addison was extraordinarily fat, weighing about 360 pounds. Both men were eccentrics, although of the two, Addison was the more stable. He frowned on many of Wilson's escapades, but did his best to protect him and admired his talents.

Addison was an architect and was famous for the beautiful neo-Spanish buildings he designed in Palm Beach and Boca Raton, Florida. Personally he was full of idiosyncrasies. A man who sometimes wore his bathrobe to the office and who kept monkeys, otters, raccoons and anteaters in the private zoo attached to his home, he liked to walk around Palm Beach with a monkey and a macaw clinging to each shoulder, and as a boy had kept a wolf as a pet. Afraid that the beast would catch cold, he slept with it every night.

The Mizner brothers were members of a prominent California family of diplomats, clergymen and lawyers who lived in Benicia, a town about thirty miles northeast of San Francisco. Addison's and Wilson's father, Lansing Bond Mizner, was a well-known politician and lawyer who also served as U. S. Minister to Guatemala, Nicaragua, Honduras, El Salvador and Costa Rica. The Mizners were Benicia's reigning family. They drank tea in the afternoon, an unheard-of custom, and were also the first family in town to have a modern toilet. In his autobiography, *The Many Mizners*, Addison recalled seeing hundreds of townspeople waiting patiently in line outside their home to see it "flush."

Addison, born in 1872, and Wilson, born in 1876, were the youngest members of the family, a large one which included four older brothers and a sister, Mary Ysabel. Since there were so many children competing for attention, brevity of speech was essential around the family dinner table. A Mizner had to learn how to say what was on his mind quickly; otherwise, he might never get a chance to say it at all. According to Addison, everyone in the family liked to cap remarks, and "unless you happened to be the wittiest, you were vanquished and driven into silence."

The brothers' sense of humor was inherited from both parents. According to Wilson, his mother "had a streak of wit like lightning, though always kind." Their father was considered one of the great extemporaneous talkers of his day, but he also believed in the simple answer. Once, during a banquet at which a banker gave a speech that droned on for hours, Lansing was asked by the toastmaster what qualities he thought made a great banker. "Circumcision," Lansing replied and immediately sat down.

When Wilson was sixteen, he ran away from home. A couple of weeks later, he wired his mother to send him five hundred dollars. She wired back, "Sorry I did not receive your telegram." Although Wilson was disappointed, he was proud of her just the same. "I knew that the son of a mother that smart was never going to starve," he said.

Both Wilson and Addison worshiped their mother. "I had a special virtue in being able to make my mother laugh hard," Wilson once wrote. "How precisely I can remember the look—the beam of her eyes, into which tears would come, made of laughter. Never was there so kind and perfect a friend of mine anywhere."

In his youth, as in his adulthood, Wilson was a rebel. After the family's return from Guatemala, he was sent to—and expelled from—Bates Preparatory School in California and then sent to Santa Clara, a reform school where the discipline was as strict as a penitentiary's. If anyone misbehaved at Santa Clara, he wasn't kicked out, but locked up in solitary for long periods of time. Every night, vicious guard dogs were let loose in the schoolyard to keep the boys from running away. One night Wilson stole some steaks from the school kitchen and tied them to a rope that led to an alarm bell. After lights-out the dogs were let out of their kennels. Pandemonium soon broke loose as the animals jumped for the raw steaks and simultaneously the alarm started ringing wildly. Wilson later stole from the gym a heavy iron ball of the sort used for shot-putting, put it in a hot stove for twenty minutes and then rolled it in the path of a priest who made the mistake of picking it up. After that he bade adieu to Santa Clara. "Imagine being expelled from a penitentiary!" Addison remarked.

Occasionally Wilson would persuade Addison to be his partner in crime. One day, a politician named Griswold came out West to help their father campaign for Benjamin Harrison, whose term as president Wilson said was "fitted in between the two terms of Grover Cleveland like a withered pickle between two pieces of homemade bread." Griswold stayed in one of the family's guest cottages. Soon the Mizner brothers went to spy on him. "He had just finished shaving," Addison later recalled. "To our horror, we saw him powder his face. No resident of Benicia could get away with that. The worst was yet to come—he used perfume on his handkerchief!" Determined to make a man out of this dandy from the East, the brothers sneaked into his room while he was out and swiftly replaced the face powder with sugar. As for the perfume, they poured most of it down the drain and then, as Addison delicately put it, "from a 'spicket' that we had with us, we filled the bottle. It was the same in color, if not in aroma."

Lansing Mizner died shortly after Wilson was expelled from Santa Clara. Although Wilson received some money from his father's estate, it was not nearly enough to support his already extravagant tastes. He began knocking about the country—singing in dives on the Barbary Coast and doing some professional boxing. He proved to be such an accomplished fighter that he became a sparring partner for Jim Corbett, Bob Fitzsimmons and Jack Johnson, all at one time or another heavyweight champions. Johnson always said that Wilson would have made a first-rate fighter had it not been for his pipestem legs.

Wilson also went to work in a medicine show, selling a concoction called "Dr. Slocum's Sweet Vermifuge Mastodon Medicine," which was said to cure everything from tapeworms to "a faltering heart." Mizner was useful to Dr. Slocum, a wiry man in a black sombrero and wide necktie, because he spoke Spanish. "Dr. Slocum regarded Latin as a first aid to credulity," Wilson told Edward Dean Sullivan, one of his biographers, "and whenever there was a restless stirring in a listening group or departures from the ranks I lapsed into Spanish with some such statement as 'in the great universities of the East—particularly New York College—we find universal satisfaction with this great remedy.' I had a great anatomical chart behind me and with my cane I would point out parts of the human machine identifying them in Spanish profanity. Dr. Slocum considered it very indelicate to mention bodily parts or functions in English."

Wilson's career with Dr. Slocum ended when his uncle, Eugene Semple, former governor of the Washington Territory, got wind of what he was doing and sent Addison to bring the wanderer home. When Addison found him, Wilson was managing Dr. Slocum's fighting bear, who had become famous in Montana because no dog could beat him in the ring. Wilson was making money betting on the bear and told Addison that he would go back to San Francisco only after the bear fought a bout against a dog named Breen. According to Alva Johnston's account in his biography of the brothers, *The Legendary Mizners*, "at the Montana town, the Breen following appeared so confident that Wilson became worried and demanded a look at the challenger. He and Addision were led to a dark stable, where they dimly made out a big, terrifically snarling animal. 'He's a tough-looking hound,' Wilson whispered to Addison, 'but he won't last a minute with my bear.' Wilson and Addison bet their last nickel on their entry. The gong sounded. The challenger charged into the ring. The bear roared and assumed its fighting pose. Instead of closing in, the two contestants paused, sniffed, and looked each other over. Suddenly, they seized each other with woofs of affection. Breen turned out to be an attractive young she-bear, and the champion couldn't be induced to lift a paw to her save in the way of kindness. At the end of three minutes, the stakeholders, despite Wilson's and Addision's protests, handed over the money to Breen's backers. The two brothers were completely cleaned out, but Addison had two tickets to San Francisco, and they took the next train home."

Wilson's next adventure led him to the Klondike. In 1897, he went to the Yukon with his older brother Edgar, a mining engineer. Accompanying them was Wilson's girlfriend of the moment, Rena Fargo, a singer he had met on the Barbary Coast, who was destined to become one of the best-known entertainers of the Gold Rush with her rendition of "You wouldn't dare insult me, Sir, if only Jack were here."

The Klondike River was frozen when the party arrived, and months were spent building a boat with sails and an enormous pair of ice skates which would carry them to the gold fields. When they took it out for its maiden voyage, however, deep snow covered the river, and both skating and sailing were impossible.

Discouraged, Wilson went to work in a Dawson City saloon, where he dealt faro and weighed gold dust which the miners used to pay their debts. Bored with these monotonous tasks, he moved on to Nome, where he joined up with underworld figures, learning to swindle at cards and then losing his winnings by gambling himself. He also ran a hotel, The McQuestion, which he liked to call "The No Questions" and soon became involved with a pretty woman named "Nellie the Pig"—so called because of her turned-up nose. "Nellie had a violent temper," he said, "and once bit off a waiter's ear, but in the main she was a lady to the knuckles of each fist."

But the fever of the Gold Rush was dwindling, and Wilson decided to go back to San Francisco. He took the long way around, going by way of Honduras, where he ran a banana plantation, and then moved on to New York. On February 2, 1906, every newspaper in New York City carried a headline on its front page saying that he and Mrs. Myra Adelaide Yerkes had gotten married. He was twenty-nine; she was the forty-eight-year-old widow of Charles T. Yerkes, the Chicago traction magnate who had built the Chicago "L," the street railway system of Philadelphia and portions of the London tube.

Mrs. Yerkes was known as "the second richest woman in the world," the first being the reclusive Hetty Green.

When Wilson met Myra, she was separated from her husband. Their separation had occurred when the millionaire became infatuated with a young actress, Emilie Grigsby, whom he liked to refer to as "his ward." Just as Yerkes was about to ask his wife for a divorce, he dropped dead of a heart attack, and since he hadn't yet changed his will, most of his estate, valued at seven and a half million dollars, went to her.

Mrs. Yerkes was not accepted by the elite of New York. Neither was Mr. Yerkes. He had served a prison term for embezzlement. As for her, she was in the habit of getting drunk and making a spectacle of herself. She would go to the theater and yell comments at the performers and then pass out in her box.

The Yerkes mansion on Fifth Avenue and 68th Street had a huge inside court with red marble columns supporting a glass dome, marble staircases, nine baths, including one of solid onyx, priceless tapestries and rooms filled with Rembrandts, Frans Halses, Vandykes and other master paintings. A powdered footman stood at the entrance. Addison, who knew Mrs. Yerkes through his millionaire connections, introduced her to his brother, and soon the powdered footman was announcing Wilson at the mansion, or "The Hut" as he called it. Several months later he and Mrs. Yerkes were married, although at first she denied to reporters that the wedding had taken place. When reporters tracked Wilson down at Sherry's and asked him if he was married, he led them to the mansion on 68th Street. "The key," he said, brandishing it and sticking it in the door. "Now, the love call," he added and suddenly yelled "Owee Owee!," a cry of the Yukon wild.

Mrs. Yerkes appeared.

"Where did you find him?" she asked the reporters. "It's more than I can do."

Unable to believe the news, Addison rushed to 68th Street. He found his brother lounging on a $35,000 bed of inlaid wood with bronze gilt appliqués that had been originally built for Mad King Ludwig of Bavaria. "At the head there was a swarm of gilt cupids covering up a seminude figure of 'Night,' and at the foot they were tearing the covers off her," Addison reported. "In the bed lay Wilson, with a woolen undershirt that had shrunk. A million dollars worth of point-lace covered him to his middle, and he was rolling a Bull-Durham cigarette in a brown paper." When Addison asked him why he had gotten married, Wilson replied, "Things are very comfortable here, and the service is excellent."

Predictably, the marriage was doomed. As soon as Wilson moved in, he turned one wing of the mansion into a training camp for boxers. The beautiful green onyx pool surrounded by medieval tapestries became a bathtub for pugilists with names like Kid Broad. Yerkes had been a collector of antique clocks, and there was a room in the mansion containing at least two thousand of them. Wilson had all the clocks wound up and delighted in showing the room to friends with hangovers, making sure that they arrived a little before striking time. He once fell asleep and was awakened by the sound of cuckooing from a big Swiss cuckoo clock on the wall of his bedroom. Reaching for a gun, he shot the cuckoo and the clock to smithereens. Myra was understandably upset.

According to Alva Johnston, "Mrs. Mizner patched up a quarrel by reenacting the big Camille scene. Mizner had left her after a financial argument. She waylaid him near an elevator in the Hotel Astor and pelted him with greenbacks. Describing this in after years, Mizner said, 'The greatest humiliation I ever underwent was picking it up.' He contradicted himself slightly in another version, saying 'I'd picked up eight thousand dollars before I realized I'd been insulted.' "

Less than a month after they were married, she sued him for divorce. Wilson emerged from the experience with one enameled modern Russian spoon. "I had never considered marriage, but I had an open mind, and I was to learn after a brief try at it that most open minds should be closed for repairs," he said.

Myra, her millions greatly diminished by lawsuits, died of alcoholism four years later. Her art treasures were sold, and the mansion demolished.

After Wilson's divorce, he ran the Rand, a seedy hotel on West 49th Street, for a few months. No one ever slept at the Rand, although Alva Johnston said that an alarm went off at three o'clock every morning, signaling guests that it was time to go back to their rooms. Wilson, as manager, devised some special rules for the clientele: "Get off at any floor and walk in any door"; "No opium smoking in elevators"; and "Guests must carry out their own dead."

The Rand's clientele consisted mostly of prostitutes. Wilson told his friends never to walk in front of the hotel if they could help it. "The girls throwing down keys to their customers will knock your brains out," he said.

The hotel boasted a small fountain which Mizner kept filled with turtles and baby alligators. Once he was arrested for throwing two men into it. When he appeared before the judge, Wilson denied the charge, saying the fountain was too small to hold two adult men. "But I'm going to enlarge it," he said.

Meanwhile, at this low point in Wilson's career, his brother Addison was thriving. In his youth Addison had also been a wanderer, but a businessman as well. He traveled extensively in the Orient, South Pacific and Central America selling coffin handles as door pulls and towel racks to the unsuspecting natives. He also stripped the great fifteenth- and sixteenth-century cathedrals of Guatemala of priceless altars, gold crosses and ecclesiastical robes which he shipped to the United States and sold at enormous profit. Finally, he turned briefly to writing, pausing long enough on one of his frequent jaunts to compose "The Cynic's Calendar," an almanac of fractured quotations.

"Be held truthful that your lies may count," "The wages of gin is breath," "Where there's a will, there's a lawsuit," and "God gives us our relatives, but thank God we can choose our friends" were a few of the homilies from this work, a great success in its day.

In New York, Addison became the rage of the Four Hundred. He was a kind of court jester to Mrs. Hermann Oelrichs, Mrs. William K. Vanderbilt, Jr. and other immensely rich women. Even Mrs. Stuyvesant Fish and her escort, Harry Lehr, were charmed by his gaiety and wit.

In his middle forties, convinced that he was dying of a rare orthopedic disease, Addison went to Palm Beach, Florida, to lie in the sun and enjoy what little time he thought he had left. At the resort he met the sewing machine magnate Paris Singer, who had also come there to die—although his symptoms were mostly caused by the heartbreak over the end of his romance with Isadora Duncan. Although Addison had once remarked that "Isadora Duncan is a bore when drunken," he took up with Singer, and the two men, greatly revived by their friendship and some weeks in the sun, decided to rebuild Palm Beach.

Addison loved the Spanish Renaissance period with its Moorish influences and went to great lengths to make his romantic fairytale creations such as the Everglades Club in Palm Beach and The Cloister in Boca Raton look old. To achieve this atmosphere, he doused rooms with soot to give them a murky look, cracked expensive mantelpieces in half and then glued the pieces together again, and jabbed furniture with an ice pick to create fake wormholes. He thought nothing of knocking off the toes, arms, noses and heads of statues. Bright colors offended him. Once, after hanging the Renaissance portrait of a cardinal in one of his Spanish mansions, he returned a few days later and said, "That son-of-a-bitch's hat is too red!"

While Addison was busy vandalizing statues and omitting staircases in some of his houses because he thought they looked better without them, Wilson had left the Rand and was writing for the stage. On the side he managed Stanley Ketchel, then the middleweight champion of the world. Ketchel's most famous fight was against Jack Johnson. Johnson weighed 200 pounds, Ketchel 160, and he knocked Johnson down in the twelfth round before being knocked out himself. Ketchel was later killed at the age of twenty-three on a ranch in Missouri by a jealous foreman who resented his attention to the pretty young housekeeper on the place.

Wilson's new profession—playwrighting—soon absorbed all his talents. There was one problem, however. He hated to write. "It's too damn lonesome," he said. He preferred to talk. "Conversation was Wilson's hobby, profession and neurosis," says Alva Johnston. What few examples we have of Wilson's work are mainly the result of somebody painstakingly recording his words on paper. According to Johnston, "with all his raffishness, he had a superiority and independence of spirit like that other disreputable aristocrat, Sir John Falstaff, who sharpened his wit on princes . . . Humorous writers comment chiefly on topics and events that go out of date almost immediately; Mizner commented on human behavior, which does not become outmoded. Mizner specialized in exposing himself, so he had an ever-ready and vulnerable butt for his wit. He had one further advantage: using the oral medium, he could freely coin phrases, for which rival wits, using the printed medium, would have gone to jail."

Like most superb raconteurs, Wilson required listeners. Johnston says that he had a sprinkler installed on top of his favorite speakeasy which he secretly asked the waiter to turn on whenever there was a lull in the conversation. Thinking that it was raining, his listeners would stay several hours more.

Wilson obviously needed a collaborator. His first one was a successful playwright named George Bronson-Howard. Together, they wrote *The Only Law*, a realistic study of criminals, which was produced in 1909 and wasn't a success. Bronson-Howard hated Mizner and described him as "a giant

Brownie—a huge head shaped like a coal scuttle, a heavy round stomach, and the thinnest legs and smallest of feet, which, in one more than six feet tall, made him something of a monstrosity."

His next collaborator was Paul Armstrong, another of Broadway's leading playwrights. Together, they wrote *The Deep Purple*, the first play to deal realistically with crooks. It was a hit, although some of the critics were scandalized by its frankness. Wilson said of a critic who attacked it, "If that fellow can criticize a play, I can make a watch that will give milk." His second play with Armstrong, *The Greyhound*, was less successful, and Mizner, by then bored with writing, dissolved the partnership. As with many collaborators, the two men spent the rest of their lives disagreeing about who had written what line and privately telling friends that he had done the lion's share of the work. Wilson had the last word. When Paul Armstrong died prematurely and the eulogy was being delivered at his funeral, Wilson whispered to a friend, "If Paul was up and about, he'd say that speech was his."

After *The Greyhound*, Mizner got a job as a screenwriter for a New York-based film company. But it was getting harder and harder to write. He had developed a drug habit, using heroin, opium and cocaine, or "snow." Once a man came into a hotel room where he was playing cards, his coat covered with snowflakes. "I've never seen a snowstorm like this," he said to Wilson. "Sir," Wilson replied, "take my nose and hang it out the window."

In the early 20s, this dependence on drugs became so bad that Addison came for him and took him down to Palm Beach, where Wilson tried desperately to break himself of the habit. He was moderately successful, although on occasion he could not resist fixing himself a liquid breakfast of alcohol and laudanum.

In the late 1920s Florida was in the middle of a real estate boom. Americans were buying up property for speculation as fast as they could. With the exception of Palm Beach, a playground for the very rich, the state was then mostly wild and uninhabited, with bogs and mangrove swamps full of alligators and poisonous snakes. Yet, in the imaginative words of the real estate ads, it was a utopia soon to be filled with gleaming cities, skyscraper hotels, thousands of beautiful homes and movie studios more lavish than any in Hollywood. Some promoters sold lots that were underwater and some advertised property in the "heights," land roughly two feet higher than the swamp adjoining it.

Realizing that a fortune could be made, the brothers formed the Mizner Development Corporation. Addison was president, Wilson director. Together, they built the world's shortest highway, El Camino Real, a twenty-lane road with a Venetian-type "Grand Canal" in the middle that ran from the Dixie Highway to Lake Boca Raton, a distance of slightly less than half a mile. Addison's beautiful Moorish "Cloister" became the Boca Raton Hotel. There was a church and several other striking edifices. Addison's dream was to build a small ornate cathedral in honor of his mother who had died at the age of eighty. But his dream remained unrealized. In 1925 the bubble burst. One of the Mizners' most influential backers, General T. Coleman du Pont, felt that the Mizners and their press agent, Harry Reichenbach, were making claims they could not substantiate. After publicly denouncing their methods as unscrupulous, he withdrew from the partnership. Sales instantly fell off. Addison's problems were compounded by the fact that his neo-Spanish architectural style was beginning to be considered passé. Georgian and Colonial reproductions were taking its place.

By 1926 the brothers were penniless. The boom was over.

The few buildings that had been constructed were destroyed by a severe hurricane in September of that year. Lawsuits were filed against them, though even here Wilson retained his wry humor. "I did not tell this man that he could grow nuts on that land," he informed a judge at one of the hearings. "I told him he could go nuts on it."

Addison remained in Palm Beach, vainly trying to pay off the debts of the company and living off loans from well-to-do friends. Wilson went to Hollywood, where he became a screenwriter as well as part owner of the Brown Derby. His partner was Herb K. Somborn, former husband of Gloria Swanson. Wilson named the restaurant in honor of Governor Alfred E. Smith, who had pardoned him after he was convicted of running a gambling house in Mineola, New York. The Governor's political trademark was a brown derby.

Wilson returned to Florida only once after the crash. What he saw upset him terribly. "I saw the vast subdivisions lining the roadsides and their massive and once ornate gates sagging in rust . . . I saw miles of cement sidewalks lined with 'White Way' lights which had nothing to be illuminated for—perhaps for years to come," Edward Dean Sullivan quoted him as saying. "I saw gaping structures tragically incomplete and a thousand reminders of boasts that never became golf courses, country clubs or casinos. I saw drunken street signs that hung feebly to their lamp posts, indifferent to whether you ever knew that Ponce de Leon Boulevard and Alcazar Avenue met."

He returned to Hollywood and resumed his screenwriting career. But he was not the same Wilson Mizner. Although his tongue was still sharp, he had aged and grown heavy. "He now had a horse face. He seemed like an immense leprechaun who must laugh at a world that deserved tears," said his friend Jim Tully.

During the day he spent most of his time at the Warner Brothers studio, sleeping. He worked on one of the early talkies, *One Way Passage*, and wrote the dialogue for *Winner Take All* and *Dark Horse*. Wilson usually slept through story conferences. When the script called for dialogue, his fellow screenwriters would shake him, make him start to talk, and then write down what he said.

In 1933, he awoke to the sound of knocking. A messenger handed him a telegram from Addison saying that he was dying. Wilson immediately wired back, "Stop dying. Am trying to write a comedy."

But Wilson himself was in frail health. He was growing deaf and wired Addison about his condition. Another man might have sympathized, but Addison, sick as he was, wired back, "What do you care? You've heard everything."

The brothers' responses to each other in these final days seem strange under the circumstances, curiously devoid of feeling. But the bond between them was powerful, almost mystic. Addison died in February 1933, and a few weeks later Wilson suffered a heart attack. Even then he could not resist a wisecrack. As he was being taken to the hospital, he was asked if he wanted a priest. "I want a priest, a rabbi and a Protestant clergyman," he said. "I want to hedge my bets."

A month later he suffered a relapse. This time a priest was summoned. "I've been talking to your boss, Father," Mizner told him. "Please try to be serious, Mr. Mizner," the priest replied. "You might have but a few hours to live."

"What?" quipped Mizner. "No two weeks' notice?"

He died of a second heart attack on April 3, 1933. He was fifty-seven years old.

A quipster and sporting man to the end, he gripped the hand of his physician as he was dying, grinned and murmured, "Well, Doc, I guess this is the Main Event."

9

Tallulah

"Anyway, cocaine isn't habit-forming, dahling, and I ought to know. I've been taking it all my life."

AS A young woman, Tallulah Bankhead was extraordinarily beautiful. She was small and slender, with a rose-petal complexion, masses of wavy honey-blonde hair and a voluptuous mouth. She came from an old aristocratic Alabama family. Her father, William Bankhead, was Speaker of the U.S. House of Representatives from 1936 to 1940.

Tallulah's childhood was strange and filled with drama. Born in Huntsville, Alabama, on January 31, 1902, she was christened next to the open coffin of her mother, Ada, a beautiful young Alabama belle who had died of blood poisoning following Tallulah's birth. Her father, crazed with grief, had chosen, bizarrely, to have the christening take place during the funeral. After his wife died, William Bankhead suffered from a deep depression which he often tried to ease with alcohol. Then a struggling young lawyer, he was given to violent tirades when drunk and sometimes ran around the house, waving a pistol and threatening to kill himself so he could join his wife in the grave. Finally, he sent the infant Tallulah and her older sister, Eugenia, to live with relatives in a nearby town. For several years he could scarcely bear the sight of his little daughter, whom he believed responsible for his wife's death.

When Tallulah became a successful actress, she reportedly never went on stage without first kneeling in front of a framed picture of her mother and praying, "Dear God, don't let me make a fool of myself tonight." After this, she would drink a glass of champagne.

Although she maintained that she was unaffected by her mother's death, her behavior throughout her life seems to indicate that the opposite was true. She had a dread of being abandoned and hated being alone. As a child she compensated for her loneliness by overeating. Her father nicknamed her "Dutch" because she was so fat, and this unflattering nickname added to her sense of inferiority.

Eugenia was their father's favorite. Affectionately he nickenamed this fragile and pretty girl "Nothin' Much" and "Kildee" after a plover, because she was so delicate and petite. This favoritism was not lost on Tallulah. To make people notice her, she threw temper tantrums, kicking her heels on the floor and howling inconsolably for hours. Grandmother Bankhead would finally lose patience and pour buckets of cold water over her. They served only to make Tallulah scream louder.

Her relatives were always comparing her to the ladylike Eugenia. As a small child, Tallulah suffered from croup, and a mustard plaster was applied to her chest, burning her skin. "Burn sister, too! Burn sister, too!" she screamed.

Her love-hate relationship with Eugenia lasted into adulthood. She once described Eugenia in a long chain of four-letter words, and then abruptly ended the sentence with, " . . . but she's good company."

The Bankheads sent Tallulah to a series of private girls' schools. She was scarcely a model student, biting her teachers on their hands when they reprimanded her, flinging inkpots against the wall and turning cartwheels at prim school functions. Instead of studying, she read screen magazines and stood for hours in front of a mirror making herself up to look like the smoldering-eyed vamps of the period. She was often expelled at the end of the semester.

During her adolescence, her father remarried. His second wife was Florence McGuire, a pretty twenty-five-year-old. Although Eugenia returned home to live with the newlyweds, Tallulah refused to go and was sent to live with her grandparents.

At fifteen, she suddenly became a raving beauty. Her complexion cleared and through rigorous dieting she became reed-slender. She and not her sister was now the belle of the family. In 1917 she entered a beauty contest sponsored by *Picture-Play* magazine, and won. Grandmother Bankhead talked her father into letting her go to New York. "I'm subsidizing Tallulah, Will. Let her go on the stage. She's not worth a damn for anything but acting." Within a few months after arriving in New York with her Aunt Louise, Tallulah moved into the Algonquin. It was the city's most famous theatrical hotel, and much patronized by intellects and wits of the day. Aunt Louise picked it, however, according to Tallulah, because it was the New York headquarters of Commander Evangeline Booth of the Salvation Army. She added, "Whatever the reason, her choice was providential. At once I was rubbing elbows with the theater's great and notorious. I'll never forget the first night we walked into the dining room. At various tables were seated Texas Guinan, the Talmadge sisters, Laurette Taylor and Douglas Fairbanks."

The wits of the Algonquin were charmed by the new arrival. She was so pretty and naive and so in love with the theater. "Tallulah was crowding seventeen when she arrived from Alabama," wrote Margaret Case Harriman in her book *The Vicious Circle*. "She was stage-struck, sultry-voiced, and brimming with a roseleaf beauty which she determinedly hid under the then-fashionable mask of white powder, blue eye-shadow, and beef-colored lipstick. She fondly believed that this made her look like Ethel Barrymore, who was her idol." Tallulah had only one dress, a black one, and when it was being cleaned, she had to stay in her room.

One evening, soon after her arrival, she was taken to the theater by Alexander Woollcott to see a play by Maurice Maeterlinck. Tense and nervous in the famous drama critic's company, she had said, "There's less in this than meets the eye," when all she had intended was the timid comment, "There's more in this than meets the eye." Woollcott was so amused he quoted it in his column.

Soon she had the reputation of being a considerable wit, although her remarks had none of the polish and deadly malice of a Dorothy Parker. Essentially exhibitionistic, Tallulah's wit—like her habit of taking her clothes off at parties—was designed for only one purpose, to make people notice her. As Lee Israel pointed out in her biography, *Miss Tallulah Bankhead*, "Tallulah's wit issued only from her need to make people laugh, or shudder, or react. If it was cynical and shocking, it was mostly because cynicism and shock worked for her."

At age twenty Tallulah's wisecracks were entirely hit-or-miss. She simply opened her mouth and let things come out.

She loved to talk. She talked while she ate, read a book, made love, even while she went to the bathroom. "Most of the wisecracks I have mothered have been accidental quips," she said. "Anyone who talks as much and as long as I do is sure to come up with some howlers. More than one companion has quailed under the impact of 'I never eat on an empty stomach,' 'I've had six juleps and I'm not even sober,' and 'We're reminiscing about the future.' Then there's the night I blurted my way into a boner at the Stork Club. I had a tentative appointment with Herbert Agar, following a Freedom House rally. We were to have a drink together could he get away in time. When Mr. Agar did not show up at the agreed hour, about to depart I turned to the major-domo and said: 'Should Mr. Agar come in, tell him I've gone home to bed and he may join me there.' "

Tallulah's fashionable friends learned to listen for such remarks and repeated them among the smart circles of the day.

Tallulah occasionally matched wits with Dorothy Parker, but Dorothy was usually the victor. At a party one night Tallulah got drunk and turned some cartwheels before being taken home to bed. "Oh, has Whistler's mother gone?" asked Dorothy after she had left. The next day, when Tallulah was told about her remark, she replied, "The less I behave like Whistler's mother, the more I look like her the next morning."

Tallulah began her acting career with a walk-on part in *The Squab Farm,* which was panned. Parts in more bad plays followed. Heywood Broun, no doubt fascinated by his own linguistic gifts, wrote, "Don't look now, Tallulah, but your show is slipping." Fortunately, about this time she attracted the attention of Sir Gerald Du Maurier, a famous English director and actor (Daphne Du Maurier's father), who brought her to London and cast her in a series of plays which made her reputation abroad.

Soon she became a kind of cult figure in England, with hundreds of women waiting patiently in line for thirty hours or more to buy tickets to her shows and other dyeing their hair honey-blonde and wearing the same style of dresses she strolled about in on stage. Her sultry manner and husky voice were much admired by Winston Churchill, the Aga Khan and Lawrence of Arabia. She had many lovers, but never worried about her promiscuity. "I'm as pure as the driven slush," she liked to say.

She lived in a luxurious flat and bought herself a Bentley. But since she often got lost in London, she hired a taxi to lead the way when she drove the car.

In London she met the man she called the love of her life—Lord Napier Alington, a man wracked by tuberculosis. Napier had a habit of suddenly disappearing and not being heard of for months. Sometimes he would hail a London taxi, ride to Dover, cross the Channel and continue on to Paris and Venice. Tallulah adored him, although they quarreled incessantly. She described their relationship as "part ecstasy, part torture." She longed to marry him, but he never asked her, and the wife he chose was the sedate daughter of an earl.

Perhaps even for Napier, her antics were a trifle wild. "I'm the foe of moderation, the champion of excess," she liked to say and set about to prove it. She bobbed her long blonde hair, causing Du Maurier to weep, and turned cartwheels on stage in mid-performance when a tiny monkey on her shoulder snatched off her black wig. At parties she began to be famous for taking off her clothes at a moment's notice. Once when Prime Minister Ramsay MacDonald and his spinster sister came backstage to see her, a Dr. Jones was announced. Politely, the MacDonalds offered to leave, but Tallulah cried, "Oh, don't go. I want you to meet him. He's the best abortionist in town."

Like Napier, Tallulah had lovers of both sexes, although according to Lee Israel, "by the time she reached her middle twenties, she had decided that she liked men better than women or at least she like the *idea* of men better than women." Yet, nothing delighted her more than to nettle women she disliked with insinuations of deviant sexual conduct. At parties she enjoyed flinging her arms around a conventional-looking woman and exclaiming, "Dahling, don't you know I'm just mad about you!" Once she was interviewed at her hotel by a woman reporter she detested. After the interview, Tallulah walked her to the elevator. "Lovely seeing you, dahling," she called out after the reporter had stepped into a crowded elevator and its doors began to close, "you're one of the nicest dykes I know."

Only her beauty enabled her to get away with such behavior. Augustus John painted her; Dorothy Wilding and Cecil Beaton photographed her. In a piece of florid prose, Beaton described how she looked at the peak of her beauty. "Tallulah is a wicked archangel, with her flowing ash-blonde hair and carven features. Her profile is perfectly Grecian, flow of line from forehead to nose, like a head on a medallion. She is Medusa, very exotic with a gorgeous skull, high pumice-stone cheek bones and a broad brow, and she was equally interesting sculpturally when she was plump as she now is cadaverously thin." But Beaton was not yet finished with his tone poem. "Her cheeks are huge acid-pink peonies," he continued. "Her eyelashes are built out with hot liquid paint to look like burnt matches, and her sullen, discontented rosebud of a mouth is painted the brightest scarlet, and is as shiny as Tiptree's strawberry jam."

In 1931 Tallulah returned to the United States to make five pictures for Paramount at fifty thousand dollars apiece. She was promoted as the second Marlene Dietrich—the German-born actress was then in vogue—but none of her films was a success. Neither were the next three plays she starred in. One, a comedy, opened on the very day in March 1933 when all the banks in the country were closed by incoming president Franklin Delano Roosevelt.

During rehearsals for *Jezebel,* Tallulah was suddenly taken ill and had to be replaced in the part by Miriam Hopkins. Doctors diagnosed the cause of her illness as a severe peritoneal infection, caused by an untreated case of gonorrhea. They had to perform several operations, including a total hysterectomy. She was deeply humiliated, but tried to make light of the misfortune. "Don't think this has taught me a lesson," she said as she tottered from the hospital.

In 1937, attending a performance of *Busman's Holiday,* she fell in love with the star, a John Barrymore look-alike named John Emery. Less than two months later they were married at the family home in Jasper, Alabama. Tallulah was thirty-five, her bridegroom thirty-two.

Tallulah's sister Eugenia was married seven times (three times to the same man), while Tallulah's marriage to Emery lasted only four years. When they were divorced, Emery summed up their union by saying, "It was like the rise, decline and fall of the Roman empire."

They appeared in one show together—*Anthony and Cleopatra.* The critics panned it unanimously. Richard Watts, Jr., said that Tallulah was "rather more a serpent of the Sewanee than of the Nile," and John Mason Brown wrote, "Tallulah Bankhead barged down the Nile last night as Cleopatra—and sank."

Despite her notices, Tallulah was well on her way to becoming a legend in the American theater, a cult figure as she had been in Great Britain. "I don't care what they say, as long as they talk about me" was her slogan. She was certainly talked about. To fail to notice her was like failing to notice an earthquake. She never stopped talking from morning till midnight. Her personal habits were as amazing as her interminable monologues. She smoked five packages of cigarettes a day and downed a quart of Old Grand-Dad bourbon. If the play she was starring in was dull, she would liven things up by turning cartwheels. Later, when after-theater parties were duller still, she'd turn cartwheels without her underpants on. At gatherings in her country home, she would drape herself on top of the piano and sing "Bye-Bye Blackbird," wearing only a string of pearls. This habit of undressing led her friend, actress Estelle Winwood, to say, "I don't understand Tallulah. She has so many pretty frocks."

Merv Griffin remembers that Tallulah was nude when he met her, and she invited Tennessee Williams to walk into her bathroom while she was taking a bath. Even so distinguished a visitor as Mrs. Eleanor Roosevelt was treated in an unorthodox manner. While they were having tea at Tallulah's, the actress had to go to the bathroom. Rather than miss a single word of the conversation, she left the bathroom door ajar. With perfect aplomb Mrs. Roosevelt went on talking and drinking tea.

Not everyone approved of Talluah. "Tallulah is always skating on thin ice," said Mrs. Patrick Campbell, the British actress. "Everyone wants to be there when it breaks." Howard Dietz, the songwriter, quipped, "A day away from Tallulah is like a month in the country." Walter Slezak, the Viennese actor, found listening to her constant chatter like a Chinese water torture. She and Slezak acted together late in her career in the Alfred Hitchcock film *Lifeboat*, and Slezak was particularly annoyed by Tallulah's habit of lifting her skirt armpit-high when she climbed in and out of the lifeboat so that everyone could see that she wasn't wearing underpants.

In 1939, Tallulah finally found a stage role suited to her

gifts. It was the part of the conniving mercenary Regina Giddens in Lillian Hellman's play about the South, *The Little Foxes.* The critics raved over her, and the play ran for 408 performances. But Tallulah took umbrage at Hellman's political views and angrily remarked, "I say she's spinach and I say the Hellman with her." This play on words was inspired by a 1928 *New Yorker* cartoon drawn by Carl Rose, in which a pretty little girl offered a dish of broccoli by her mother says rebelliously, "I say it's spinach and I say the hell with it."

After that Tallulah and Lillian Hellman did not speak to each other for twenty-seven years.

Tallulah didn't care for Bette Davis very much either. "When I heard that Bette Davis was playing me in *All About Eve,* I said, 'Hasn't she always?' " she once wrote. She was undoubtedly piqued because Bette had been cast in three of the film roles Tallulah had created on the stage—*Jezebel, Dark Victory* and *The Little Foxes.* Recently Bette Davis told a *Time* magazine reporter, "Tallulah once came up to me at a party and said, 'You took three parts away from me. And I played them all so much better than you did.' I looked at her and said, 'I agree.' She simply melted out of the room . . . She always insisted that Margo Channing in *All About Eve* was based on her. It's not true; Margo wasn't based on any single person. But there was a resemblance when I made the movie. I had laryngitis, and it gave me the same croaky voice that she had."

As Tallulah was about to go on tour with *The Little Foxes,* her father collapsed just as he was about to make a political speech. Doctors found that his abdominal artery had ruptured. Tallulah and her sister rushed to the hospital. While they were standing beside their father's bed, a doctor entered and asked him, "Where is the pain?" Mr. Bankhead answered strangely, "I don't play favorites. I scatter my pain." Many years later Tallulah was to write, "Just before we parted, I leaned over and kissed his cheek. 'Daddy, do you still love me?' I asked. He flashed his winning smile. 'Why talk about circumferences?' he answered."

Haunted by the ambiguity of her father's mysterious replies, Tallulah returned to New York. Shortly after she left him, William Bankhead died. He was given a state funeral in the chamber of the House of Representatives where he served for twenty-three years. Less than a month later, Napier Alington, who had become a fighter pilot in the Royal Air Force—"the only love of Tallulah's life"—was killed at the age of forty-three in the Battle of Britain. At about the same time Tallulah and John Emery were divorced.

These three events combined to mark a definite change in her life. Although she acquired another plum starring role as Sabrina in Thornton Wilder's fantasy, *The Skin of Our Teeth*, her private behavior became increasingly unrestrained. All her life her father had acted as her conscience. He loathed profanity, and she never used foul language in front of him. She had gone to elaborate pains to keep him from learning about her wildest escapades. But now that he was dead, she did exactly as she pleased, and what she pleased was more and more outrageous.

Her quips became coarse and earthy. When sex researcher Dr. Alfred Kinsey asked her to tell him all about her sex life, she retorted, "Naturally, but you must tell me all about yours first." Once she was in a ladies room and found herself without toilet paper. She called to the lady in the next booth, "Sorry to bother you, dahling, but do you have any toilet paper?" "Afraid not," said the woman. "Well, then, dahling," Tallulah replied, "do you have two fives for a ten?"

Backstage her strident quarrels with colleagues multiplied. At a party she threw all the shoes of the women guests into the street. For years she had adored animals, but now her feelings for them intensified. "Oh my God, I've killed it!" she screamed at breakfast after dropping an egg into a frying pan. To her sizable menagerie she added a Shetland pony, a golden marmoset and a myna bird who screeched "Birds can't talk!" There was also Gaylord, a budgerigar parrot who liked to perch on the rim of brandy snifters and dip his beak into people's cognac. After she and Emery were divorced, she adopted a lion cub named Winston—named for Winston Churchill, whom she greatly admired. Winston the lion cub traveled with her, and even appeared on stage, much to the consternation of her fellow actors. When Winston reached puberty and started swiping at reporters and cast members, Tallulah reluctantly gave him to the Bronx Zoo.

She could not bear to be alone for even an hour and suffered intensely from insomnia. To keep her company, she hired paid male companions, homosexual "caddies" who drew her bathwater, shaved to a perfect degree of sharpness her favorite brand of lipstick (Elizabeth Arden's "Victory Red") and kept her supplied with her daily cigarettes, liquor and pills. All of the caddies were young, and most of them adored her, recalling her jokes and eccentric ways long after her death. One of their most important duties was to hold her hand until she drifted off to sleep, usually in the early hours of the morning. They also knew never to embrace her, for although Tallulah was always kissing and hugging her friends and lovers, she could not bear any reciprocation. Some of her caddies thought her horror of being touched was caused by her barbiturate addiction, which can make the skin exquisitely sensitive; others believed it stemmed from feelings of deep insecurity—she was not worthy of being kissed—while still others felt that Tallulah was afraid that any person who touched her might assume dominance over her.

Even in her decline, her tongue was still caustic. "Dahling," she said to Tennessee Williams after seeing the movie version of his play *The Rose Tattoo,* "dahling, they've gone and *ruined* that terrible play of yours!" One day she dropped a fifty-dollar bill into the tambourine of a Salvation Army volunteer and said, "Don't bother to thank me. I know what a perfectly *ghastly* season it's been for you Spanish dancers." When a guest at her house woke up, he was immediately served a big tumbler of gin. "What's this for?" he asked. Tallulah yelled back from a neighboring bedroom, "Better drink it, dahling. I warn you there won't be another round served before breakfast."

Columnist Earl Wilson, who has a high-pitched voice, once telephoned Tallulah. "Are you ever mistaken for a man on the phone?" he asked. "No dahling," she drawled in her husky voice. "Are you?"

She owned jewels worth a fortune but seldom wore them. "I hate to get dressed up unless I'm paid for it," she told a friend. The only jewelry she used was a two-strand necklace of cultured pearls which she wore only to the dentist, calling them her "dentist pearls." (Proud of her beautiful teeth, Tallulah was always going to the dentist to have them cleaned.)

Her stagework as a young woman had often been brilliant, but as she grew older, she became more of a character and less of an actress. Tallulah performed seldom in her later years. When she did, audiences, knowing her reputation for bizarre behavior and remarks, often began hooting and catcalling as soon as she stepped out on stage.

In the last few years of her life she became a virtual recluse and spent most of her time playing cards or watching soap operas. Once she refused a phone call from President Harry Truman because he happened to call in the middle of her favorite TV show. Her caddies looked after her solicitously and watched her every movement, for she had an unfortunate habit of stumbling into things and cracking her ribs if she left her bed. She also smoked constantly and several times set herself and her bedclothes on fire.

Despite plastic surgery on her face and breasts, every trace of her beauty was finally gone. Orson Welles said, "She was the most sensational case of the aging process being unkind. I'll never forget how awful she looked at the end and how beautiful she looked at the beginning." Yet, she took the loss of her looks with grace, telling strangers who asked if she was really Tallulah Bankhead, "I'm what's left of her, dahling."

In 1968 she died of pneumonia complicated by emphysema. She was sixty-five. Her last intelligible words were "codeine-bourbon."

They buried her in Rock Hall, on the eastern shore of Maryland, in a small remote cemetery not far from her sister's home. She was dressed in one of her old silk robes, dotted with cigarette-burn holes. At her side was the good-luck charm which in life she had never been without—a rabbit's foot her father had given her as a present many years before.

10

Alice Roosevelt Longworth

Washington's Enfant Terrible

"If you haven't got anything good to say about anyone, come and sit by me."

"*HE SPRANG* from the grass roots of the country clubs of America," she said of Republican presidential candidate Wendell Willkie. The speaker was a slender, beautiful woman with fearless gray-blue eyes and a rapid-fire manner of talking whenever she was excited. Her wit was legendary and heavily spiked with malice. When asked her opinion of journalist Dorothy Thompson, who made a lot of money on the lecture circuit espousing her liberal philosophy, this political conservative snapped: "She is the only woman who had her menopause in public and got paid for it."

Her name was Alice Roosevelt Longworth, and although she was the daughter of Theodore Roosevelt, twenty-sixth President of the United States, she was never inclined to be a paragon of virtue and propriety. When her father forebade her to smoke "under his roof," she took his ultimatum literally and puffed happily away—*on* the roof of the White House. Nothing frightened her, not even snakes. For a time her favorite companion was a slithery green serpent named Emily Spinach—Emily in honor of an aunt who was painfully thin, and Spinach because it was green. Once, when her half-brother Quentin was ill, she cheered him up by smuggling his pony into a White House elevator and up to his sickroom. Never one to tolerate boredom, she made dreary rainy days livelier by filching tea trays from the White House pantry and sliding on them down the stairs. Years later, guests who attended T. R.'s state dinners recalled having their knees tickled by the younger Roosevelt children, begging for food. It was saucy Alice, of course, who put them up to it. At staid gatherings, she was known to fire off cap pistols and turn a back somersault or two just for the hell of it. She scandalized Victorian society by motoring alone with another girl "all the way from Newport to Boston without a chaperone." Even the colorful Theodore Roosevelt had to admit that Alice's exuberant nature sometimes overwhelmed him. "I can do one of two things," he confided to Owen Wister, the writer, who had objected to Alice's flitting in and out of her father's office while the President and Wister were talking, "I can be President of the United States or I can control Alice. I cannot possibly do both."

Alice liked to blame her tomboy behavior on her father. She said that it was from him she had inherited her love of showing off. "Father wanted to be the corpse at every funeral, the bride at every wedding, and the baby at every christening," she said of him. Like her, he was capable of a razor-sharp wit, especially if he felt ignored or was forced to play second fiddle. "McKinley has no more backbone than a chocolate éclair," he said of the chief executive under whom he served as Vice-President.

When Alice was born on Lincoln's birthday, February 12, 1884, Teddy, then a Republican assemblyman in Albany, New York, regarded it as a lucky sign. His happiness soon turned into despair, for the birth of Alice was followed by tragedy. Her mother, Alice Hathaway Lee, a willowy, hazel-eyed beauty nicknamed "Sunshine" because of her happy disposition, died of Bright's disease, a severe kidney ailment, when the baby was two days old. One day earlier, Teddy's mother, Mittie, had also died (of typhoid fever) in the same house they shared in Manhattan. "There is a curse on this house," Elliott Roosevelt cried as he opened the door for brother Teddy, who had rushed home from Albany the minute he heard that his mother was gravely ill. "Mother is dying, and Alice is dying, too!"

Teddy, who adored his pretty young wife, was inconsolable. Soon after her death, he wrote in his diary: "Fair, pure and joyous as a maiden, loving, tender and happy as a young wife. When she had just become a mother, when her life seemed to be but just begun and when the years seemed so bright before her, then by a strange and terrible fate death came to her. And when my heart's dearest died, the light went from my life forever . . ."

He never spoke of his dead wife to Alice. It was as if the beautiful girl who had been the center of his life had never even existed. His silence on the subject troubled—and deeply perplexed—his family, and affected his daughter as well. No one ever knew what motivated Teddy, but perhaps the most plausible reasoning came from Nicholas Roosevelt. He wrote: "The only rational explanation that I have heard is that T. R.'s determination to regard his first marriage and his life with Alice Lee as a chapter never to be reread was so great that he deliberately buried it in the recesses of his memory forever."

In 1886, three years after his young wife's death, Teddy married Edith Kermit Carow, a former childhood playmate he had intermittently kept in touch with for many years before he married Alice Lee. Unlike his shy, even-tempered first wife, Edith had a volatile nature. She could be sweet and helpful one day, sullen and bad-tempered the next. Soon after this second marriage, Alice went to live with her father and new stepmother at Sagamore Hill, their big rambling mansion in Oyster Bay, Long Island. The transition was not easy for a pampered three-year-old. Since her mother's death, she had been living a spoiled existence with her father's maiden sister Anna—or "Bye" as she was affectionately called.

Bye was to have a profound influence on Alice. Although she was middle-aged, plain-looking and crippled with a spinal disease, she was very much the grande dame who captivated everyone with her rare intelligence and sparkling wit. At her home in New York, she ran a sort of salon, which attracted well-known artists, writers and politicians. The night table in her bedroom was stacked high with the latest books so she could keep up with what was happening in the world. As Alice grew older, she emulated her distinguished aunt by becoming an avid reader and brilliant conversationalist. She also became pregnant when she was middle-aged—like Bye, who married late in life and had a child at forty-four. It was from Bye, too, that Alice acquired her remarkable gift for mimicry; she loved to impersonate monkeys and bears and did excellent imitations of Ethel Barrymore and President Taft's wife Nellie.

As much as Alice adored her father, Bye was the family member who really impressed her the most. "If Aunt Bye had been a man, she would have been President," she often said. Bye had another endearing attribute in Alice's eyes: she talked to the girl about her dead mother, something the other Roosevelts refused to do.

Vying with Bye for Alice's attention were the Lees, her maternal grandparents. With warm generosity, they gave her a pony and an ample trust fund, with the stipulation that she be allowed to use the interest on luxuries for herself. "There never were such kind, indulgent, affectionate grandparents—four aunts and an uncle as well—who let me have my way until I ought to have been spanked," she said. "I would celebrate my arrival by violently jumping up and down on the sofa until the springs sagged, something I should never have dreamed of doing at home . . . When the time came to go home, I used to dissolve in woe at leaving my grandmother, partly because she was dear to me and I loved her, but I fear also because I missed having the world swing about my small selfish self." Because of her trust fund, Alice soon became the richest member of the Roosevelt family and before she came to live permanently at Sagamore Hill, Teddy was reported to have cautioned Edith: "Be nice to Alice. We might have to borrow money from her one day."

Despite the attention lavished on her by Bye and her grandparents, Alice was unhappy. She found her stepmother Edith distant and inflexible, the direct opposite of her indulgent and warmhearted Bye. With four half-brothers and a half-sister, all children of Edith and Teddy, she felt like an outsider. "My brothers used to tease me about not having the same mother. I was terribly sensitive," she confided many years later to *Washington Post* reporter Sally Quinn.

Physical problems intensified her basic shyness. Like many of the Roosevelts, including her first cousin Eleanor who wore a steel brace for two years to correct a curvature of the spine, Alice suffered from orthopedic problems. To correct them, she had to wear heavy braces which extended from her ankles to her knees. Every night until she was thirteen her legs were "stretched" in a steel contraption that reminded Alice of a medieval instrument of torture.

Perhaps hoping to be miraculously cured of her affliction, Alice began to practice witchcraft in secret, burying little idols in the backyard when she was only five years old. She referred to the private spells she cast as "murrains"—plagues affecting domestic animals or plants.

When Alice was sixteen, President William McKinley asked her father to be his running mate for his second term after his first Vice-President, Garret A. Hobart, died in office. McKinley and Teddy Roosevelt won the election easily, but while other girls might have been ecstatic, Alice found herself at the inaugural parade staring coldly at President McKinley and wondering "in the terminology of the insurance companies what sort of a 'risk' he was. I had an ever-present resentment at Father's having been shoved into the vice-presidency. I know I regarded the President and poor frail little Mrs. McKinley as if they were two usurping cuckoos."

A year later, in 1901, McKinley was shot twice by anarchist Leon Czolgosz as he was shaking hands with supporters in Buffalo, New York. When Alice heard that someone had tried to assassinate him, but that he was expected to live, she said she began practicing her magic, crossing her fingers, saying her spells and burying little idols on the White House grounds.

In a week, after a bungled operation, McKinley died of an infection. Teddy's daughter feigned indifference, although later she insisted that what she really felt was "utter rapture."

Alice was in her teens when her father became President. Like him, she too had arrived: After years of pain and embarrassment, she no longer had to wear the heavy braces which had encumbered her—and she was also no longer "the rather chunky girl" she had described herself to be, but a beauty. Slim, stunning, with hair the color of amber, large blue eyes and a firm round chin, she blossomed into a graceful young lady who wore modishly cut gowns and dashing hats the size of cartwheels. Many of her dresses were made of a fabric that matched her gray-blue eyes. This shade became known as "Alice Blue" and inspired a popular song of the day, "Alice Blue Gown," written especially for her.

Alice soon became the most photographed and talked-about woman of her era. Every witticism, every escapade, every slight change of costume was duly reported in the press. Reporters christened her "Princess Alice" after a false rumor was started that the Kaiser's brother, Prince Henry of Prussia, was planning to propose. Alice always hated her nickname. Many years later when some sycophant said she was the nearest thing this country ever had to royalty, she snorted, "Oh, pish! Utter nonsense!" She also despised her name, Alice. Among her friends, only Dean Acheson was permitted to call her that; everyone else was instructed to call her "Sister" or, after she was married, "Mrs. Longworth" or "Mrs. L."

Meanwhile she continued to shock and delight the nation with her antics. Unlike her earnest, high-minded cousin Eleanor, she never involved herself in good causes and spent most of her evenings fending off admirers and twirling around a dance floor until dawn. When the automobile first came out, she was among the first women to drive one, as well as one of the first to be caught breaking the speed limit.

In the spring of 1905, she went on an "inspection tour" of the Orient with William Howard Taft, then Secretary of War. Her trip was a huge success. Not only did she meet the Empress Dowager of China and learn the intricacies of the hula from natives in Hawaii; she also managed to titillate the nation from halfway around the world by plunging into the ship's pool fully clothed. On this trip she also became romantically involved with another member of the party, a tall, prematurely bald bachelor with a luxurious silky mustache. He was Representative Nicholas Longworth of Cincinnati, who came from a prominent Ohio family and was fourteen years her senior. Soon after their return to the United States, their engagement was announced.

Alice was twenty-two, Nick thirty-six when they were married, five days after Alice's birthday, on February 17, 1906.

Their White House wedding was the social event of the season. The entire front page of the *Washington Post* was devoted to the event. Church bells pealed throughout the city on the morning of the wedding. Gifts were showered on the bridal couple from every corner of the globe and included gold brocades from the Orient, a $25,000 string of sixty-three matched pearls and a box of wriggling snakes. Alice chose not to have any attendants at the ceremony. "I didn't want any damned bridesmaids taking the attention from me," she said.

Like his new wife, Nick had a sense of humor though it was less subtle, broader and bawdier than hers. At lunch one day, a congressman jokingly ran his hands over Nick's bald pate. "It feels just like my wife's backside," the congressman said. Nick reached up and thoughtfully stroked his head. "So it does," he replied.*

Alice and Nick, though, had little in common. An accomplished violinist, he was in the habit of spending at least three nights a week playing classical music until the early morning hours. "I fiddled my way into society," he said. Alice, on the

*This remark has sometimes been attributed to the playwright Marc Connelly, who was also bald.

other hand, had no interest in good music. Her idea of a marvelous evening was to play poker until dawn. But there were far more serious differences between them. Nick had always been a confirmed ladies' man, and had no intention of changing after marriage. In fact, his extramarital liaisons were so numerous that he was known as the greatest womanizer on the Hill. Although Alice never mentioned his infidelities to her friends (whining and self-pity were against her code of ethics), she undoubtedly must have felt wounded and humiliated by his behavior. In Cincinnati, where the Longworths lived for a time, the neighbors told a story about Alice taking a stroll through the park and almost stumbling over her husband as he lay on the ground, embracing a pretty girl. According to the report, Alice pretended she had not seen them and walked swiftly away.

Although she "hardly reveled in marriage," she tried hard nevertheless to understand what drove her restless, sardonic husband. Once she wrote: "[Nick's] father had died sixteen or seventeen years before and he and his mother had a peculiarly close relationship. They were devoted to one another . . . I know how hard it was for her to have him marry at all; and I was not someone who 'merged' with the family she married into, not by a long shot, I fear. Besides being an egotist, I was too much one of my own family for that."

But divorce was out of the question. Like her father who prided himself on his fortitude, Alice firmly believed in committing oneself to a choice once it had been made. There is no evidence that she ever took a lover to compensate for Nick's neglect. But at parties she was often seen in the company of Senator William E. Borah of Idaho and later with the volcanic labor leader, John L. Lewis. At first glance, Alice Longworth and John L. Lewis might have seemed an unlikely couple. She was slender and elegant, while he was short and stocky, with heavy jowls, deep-set eyes and bushy brows. A cigar was always clenched between his teeth, and when he was angry, he jabbed at the air with a forefinger. But Lewis was iron-willed and tough like Teddy Roosevelt, and no one could be more thunderously persuasive when he was fired up about justice for the working man.

Politics, for Alice, was always her first love. She had violent likes and dislikes. When Woodrow Wilson, whom she despised, returned from the Paris Peace Conference in 1919, Alice was on the White House grounds to greet him, but unlike the other spectators, her purpose in being there was not a benevolent one. "I got out of my motor and stood on the curbstone to see the Presidential party pass, fingers crossed, making the sign of the evil eye and saying 'A murrain on him, a murrain on him, a murrain on him,' " she reported.

The year 1919 was one of the worst in Alice's life. Soon after the New Year, on January 6, Theodore Roosevelt, the person she loved most, died in his sleep. An intensely private woman, Alice, though devastated, revealed her emotions to no one. Instead, she transformed her grief into fury against her father's rival, Woodrow Wilson. With the help of some influential senators, she concentrated on attacking Wilson's cherished League of Nations proposal and was thrilled when the measure was defeated in the Senate.

Wilson and McKinley were not the only Presidents she hated. William Howard Taft, who succeeded her father, was another unfortunate over whom she cast her spells. After burying one of her malevolent little idols on the White House grounds and wishing him bad luck, within months, she seems to have accomplished her purpose: Taft's inaugural was spoiled by a blizzard, and Nell, his wife, suffered a severe stroke that impaired her speech permanently.

Nor was Alice more charitable toward Warren G. Harding,

Wilson's whiskey-drinking and poker-playing successor. Shortly after Harding's death, following the Teapot Dome scandal and the revelations about his White House mistress—she provided him with an epitaph: "I think everyone must feel that the brevity of his tenure of office was a mercy to him and to the country. Harding was not a bad man. He was just a slob."

After this statement, many a snide political remark was attributed to Alice. Calvin Coolidge was written off with the sentence: "He looks as if he had been weaned on a pickle." As for Alice's cousin Franklin, she said that everybody knew he was "one third sap, two thirds Eleanor." She was reported to have ruined Thomas E. Dewey's chances for the presidency by asking: "How can the Republican party nominate a man who looks like the bridegroom on a wedding cake?" With characteristic honesty, however, she refused to accept credit for inventing all these flatteners. She said she had merely repeated them so often she gave them "currency." For example, she insisted she had heard the remark about Coolidge at her doctor's. A patient who had just left his office had coined it, she said. "Of course I shouted with pleasure and told everyone, always carefully giving credit to the unnamed originator, but in a very short time it was attributed to me," she wrote in her autobiography *Crowded Hours*.

What she did actually say about the notoriously taciturn Coolidge was based on the fact that his wife, Grace, had once been a teacher at a school for the deaf and dumb. Alice commented, "That made it easier for her to live with Calvin."

Alice always insisted that she was not a wit. "I'm not witty. I'm funny. I'm the old firehorse. I just perform. I give a good show—just one of the Roosevelt show-offs."

When Prohibition began, Alice became one of the first bootleggers. The Longworths not only bought carloads of grapes and experimented with winemaking, but they had a small still with which their butler managed to concoct "a very passable gin from oranges." They also made beer in the basement—a beverage so tasty and refreshing that the British statesman Arthur James Balfour, on a break from the Disarmament Conference, complimented them on it, saying that beer brewed at their house was always better than beer from a brewery.

Once, at a nonalcoholic party, Alice delighted her two male dinner partners by presenting them with tiny bottles of liquor that she had managed to conceal in her long white gloves.

Nick enjoyed drinking, but Alice imbibed very little. It wasn't a moral issue, she doggedly maintained—it was simply that tipsy people were even more boring than dull ones. At dinner parties, she usually arrived late so as to bypass the cocktail hour.

At forty-one, after eighteen years of marriage, she became pregnant. "I'm always willing to try anything once," she explained. Her daughter, Paulina, was born in 1925. It was a boon year for both Longworths. Nick had just been elected Speaker of the House.

With his wife's help, Nick became a powerful and popular political figure. "Nick Longworth was considerably above the House level of intelligence," wrote Drew Pearson and Robert S. Allen in *Washington Merry-Go-Round*. They also said that Alice "not only attends the outstanding Senate debates and committee hearings, but behind the scenes she pulls the wires as far as she is able . . ."

But the one string she could not pull was the presidency. All her life she would dream that someone in her branch of the Roosevelt family might one day inhabit the White House again. But it was not to be. In 1928, Longworth seemed to come close, but the Republican party chose Herbert Clarke Hoover as its presidential nominee instead.

Three years later, in 1931, while vacationing alone in Aiken, South Carolina, Nick contracted pneumonia. Within days he was dead. Stoical as always, Alice refused to let her grief show. She had always loathed people who wallowed in self-pity ("perfect bores," she called them) and now she immersed herself in writing her autobiography, in the hope that the royalties would help pay off Nick's debts. Although her book, *Crowded Hours*, became a bestseller, she was embarrassed by it. She had not mentioned the deaths of her father, husband and half-brother Quentin, and had omitted the birth of Paulina altogether, but nevertheless she felt she had revealed far too much.

Though a born conversationalist, Alice was inclined to freeze when she had to commit words to paper. "Why the hell do I roar hilariously when I'm with her and then only smile when her copy comes through?" asked one of the editors of Alice's syndicated newspaper column, "Capital Comment," which she started writing in 1936 in order to rival "My Day," her cousin Eleanor's column. This editor was not the only one to complain about her prose. Maxwell Perkins, who had discovered Fitzgerald, Hemingway, Thomas Wolfe and many other writers, almost gave up when he tried to edit *Crowded Hours*. According to Perkins's biographer, A. Scott Berg: "On paper, Mrs. Longworth's words varied from stiff attempts at being literary to pointless chatter—often in the same paragraph. She had no sense of which observations were sharp and apt and which were not." Perkins and Alice met several times, and under Perkins's tutelage, her writing improved markedly to the point where the editor was finally able to write his friend, Elizabeth Lemmon, that "we made a silk purse out of a sow's ear with Alice Longworth's book—or she did . . . Now it's a good book. It might have been a splendid one. But we had to build up from worse than nothing."

When Perkins politely broached the subject of a sequel, Alice, to his vast relief, declined. "I shall never write another book," she said. "My vocabulary is too limited."

Alexander Woollcott disagreed. He told Noel Coward that "Mrs. L. enjoys being bitchy even more than I do. I always thought *that* was impossible." Howard Teichmann, one of Alice's biographers, tells about the time Alice was invited to Woollcott's private island in Vermont. There she was introduced to George S. Kaufman. "How did you happen to get into playwrighting?" Alice asked Kaufman. "Stringent vagrancy laws," Kaufman replied. After meeting Alice, he wrote a play, *First Lady*, produced in 1935, in which the leading character, Mrs. Lucy Chase Wayne, was obviously modeled on her. In the play Mrs. Wayne is described as "the woman who owned Washington," prompting Alice to write to the author: "Too bad property values are down these days."

After a few years, Alice and Alexander Woollcott were no longer friends. Politically she felt he was alarmingly liberal, "far left pro-Russian." Wounded, Woollcott sniped back at her by criticizing a new novel the publisher Nelson Doubleday was thinking about issuing: "Historically, it is about as faithful a history of the Revolution as would be an account of the last eight years in the White House written by Alice Longworth."

By then the long reign of the Oyster Bay Roosevelts was over, and the Hyde Park branch, ruled by her cousins Franklin and Eleanor, was in the ascendancy. Her branch was now "the out-of-season Roosevelts," as Woollcott dubbed them. "There we were—look at us—lovely creatures," admitted Alice to *New York Times* reporter Henry Brandon. "We were perfectly content. And what happens? A fifth cousin comes along and gets into the White House. Can you think of anything more distressing? We should be honest about it. There we were, swelling with pride and security, and what happens? Along comes Franklin, called by many in the family 'Feather Duster,' and hops into the Presidency. . . ."

Alice's opinion of Franklin had not changed an iota from the years when both were young, and many of their relatives had hoped they would marry. Both had been dashing and patrician-looking. But in spite of his good looks and easygoing charm, Franklin had never won Alice's heart. "He was the kind of boy whom you invited to the dance, but not the dinner," she told the writer Joseph P. Lash. "A good little mother's boy whose friends were dull, who belonged to the minor clubs and who never was at the really gay parties."

Now, at Franklin's White House parties, she was determined to show him up. In public, she persisted in referring to him as "Franklin," never as "Mr. President." According to Howard Teichmann, when Roosevelt "took the country off the gold standard, Alice arrived at a White House reception for the heads of government departments and stole the show. From her ears to her shoulders and below dangled gold Hindu earrings shaped somewhat like horns of plenty. About her neck, she wore a heavy chain of red gold from which hung a Chiriquí Indian frog in green gold. Her watch-bracelet was white gold. She even wore amber-golden side combs in her hair . . . She spoke with reporters the next day and conceded that what she had done was deliberate. 'I just wanted to show Franklin that all of the nation's gold wasn't in the vaults of Fort Knox.' "

Alice also upstaged Eleanor Roosevelt, whom she considered a timid woman, and what was worse, "a do-gooder." "I never did those things . . . they bored me," she said of Eleanor's passionate involvement with underprivileged people and noble causes. Using her gift for mimicry, she would imitate Franklin to perfection—and also "poor cousin Eleanor," with her high-pitched voice and earnest mannerisms. As for Eleanor's feelings about Alice, she once wrote to Franklin that she had seen Alice in New York "looking well but crazier than ever. I saw her this morning in Bobbie Goelet's auto quite alone with three other men! I wonder how you'd like my tearing around like that. I'm seriously thinking of taking it up, it seems to be the fashion nowadays."

Although they were cousins, the two women could not have been more different. Alice was assertive, self-confident and adventuresome, a rebel by nature who was always bent on attracting attention to herself, whereas Eleanor was retiring, painfully shy, and easily shocked. What the two shared in common was an adoration of their fathers and a feeling of having been rejected by their stepmothers. Eleanor later said of Alice, "While I always admired her, I was always afraid of her."

With Franklin's election to the presidency, Eleanor became the Roosevelt in the limelight, the center of attention, the woman everyone talked about. Even Alice's spiteful burlesque of her lost some of its savor when Eleanor asked her to perform it at a White House party. For Alice, perhaps the brightest spot in those years came in 1935, when the British writer Rebecca West wrote her impressions of Washington. "Physically, the city is dominated by the Washington Monument. One sees it when one least expects it, as one wanders about the wooded and pillared streets, its dark white shaft rising into the blue of high heaven, its shadow falling black over furlongs of sward. Intellectually, spiritually, the city is dominated by the last good thing said by Alice Roosevelt Longworth."

As time went on, Alice received fewer invitations to the White House. The reasons were obvious. After seeing Franklin driving around in the country with his mistress, Lucy Mercer, she told friends that "he deserved a summer wife because he was married to Eleanor." She also openly encouraged his secret affair with Lucy by inviting the couple frequently to her house for dinner. But even if Eleanor had not heard about this treachery, Alice would still have been persona non grata at the White House. The President had become tired of her constant cracks against the New Deal. When his son James suggested that she serve on a certain committee, he objected vehemently. "I don't want anything to do with that woman," he said.

The political climate in the 40s and 50s was not to Alice's liking. Although she approved of her old crony, Harry S. Truman, she was unimpressed by his successor, Dwight D. Eisenhower, whom she called "a nice boob." Her real foe, however, was Senator Joseph McCarthy, who once had the temerity to call her by her first name. "The policeman and the trashman may call me Alice, but you—*can—not*," she told him with asperity.

The 1950s were also times of grave personal crises. Paulina, Alice's only child, was a shy girl who had been raised by a governess. She went to Vassar but dropped out to marry Alexander Sturm in 1944. When she was twenty-six, her husband died of hepatitis. Unlike her stoical mother, Paulina Sturm gave way to terrible grief and depression which neither drugs nor her conversion to Catholicism could help. She began to suffer from severe migraine headaches for which the doctor prescribed still more potent drugs. One day, Joanna, her eleven-year-old-daughter, found her unconscious in their Georgetown home. Paulina was rushed to a hospital, but it was too late. At thirty-one, she was dead of what the coroner determined was an accidental overdose of the migraine medicine.

Although her paternal grandparents wanted Joanna to live with them, Alice refused. She was determined to bring up Joanna herself. So at the age of seventy-three, she set out to be both mother and father to her orphaned grandchild—or "mostly father," as a friend once said.

The 1960s proved better than the fifties. Her life was brightened by the presence of Joanna and by the Kennedys, who greatly admired her. Although she did not agree with their political views, "she was saved from any sort of oblivion by the Kennedys," a relative recalled. "There she was, already really an old woman, and the Kennedy people turned up and instantly fell in love with her. Those were marvelous, brilliant times, and there she was in the midst of it."

But it was Lyndon Johnson, John F. Kennedy's successor, who was really her favorite president aside from her father. "A lovely rogue elephant," she called him, and he returned the compliment in kind. Once he asked a beautiful young lady who was sitting next to him to change places with Alice. When an aide objected, whispering that "he didn't know what he was missing," Mr. Johnson replied, "Ah, but I know what I'm getting."

Alice was so charmed by Johnson that she, the staunchest of Republicans, actually voted for him. "Do you think the DAR will take my voting privileges away from me?" she asked gaily when she revealed the defection.

She could still put him in his place when she felt like it, however. When the President teased her about the broad-brimmed hat that with her huge purse was a kind of signature ("Mrs. Longworth, it's hard to kiss you under that brim"), she answered, "Yes, that's why I wear it."

It was during Johnson's administration that Jackie Kennedy married Aristotle Onassis. Although Alice admired the President's widow because of her excellent taste and cultural interests, she openly decried the match and remarked to Lady Bird Johnson, "Hasn't anyone ever warned Jacqueline Kennedy about Greeks bearing gifts?"

Always unpredictable, she was a great friend of Richard Nixon's, although she became less enthusiastic about him after Watergate. "Good unclean fun," she characterized it. Yet, even after his resignation, she continued to defend him, telling detractors, "I like him very much. I know other people don't."

For almost fifty-five years she lived in a five-story mansion on Dupont Circle. The front yard was overgrown with pachysandra and poison ivy, which in 1976 her cousin Joe Alsop finally persuaded her to destroy. The house, with its heavily draped windows and faded furnishings, seemed to most visitors like the vestige of another era. In the hall leading to the second floor were moth-eaten animal skins that Teddy Roosevelt had brought home many years ago from Africa. Alice loved to tell visitors the story about her cousin Stewart Alsop, Joe's brother, who "in a moment of facetiousness shook hands with the tiger and the paw came off in his hand." Gently, Alice took the paw from Stewart and put it on her mantel. It remained there for many years.

The house was filled with pictures that spanned many decades: a water color of the White House by John Singer Sargent, a portrait of Joanna, photographs of the long-dead Empress Dowager of China ("there's the old bird herself," Alice once said to Myra MacPherson of *The Washington Post*), and of course, Peter Hurd's portrait of Alice in one of her broad-brimmed hats. "I want to look like a nice old leather saddle," she had said to the artist when she sat for it.

In the upstairs sitting room was her chair pillow with the famous inscription in needlepoint: "If you haven't got anything good to say about anyone, come and sit by me."

This room served as an entranceway to the main sitting room where Mrs. Longworth entertained at tea almost daily. "An invitation to the White House is nice, but the real social coup in Washington is to be invited to tea at Alice Roosevelt Longworth's," Harry Reasoner told his TV audience. And what unique social occasions they were. At five o'clock, Alice, usually accompanied by Joanna, would make a grand entrance and greet her guests. Susan Sheehan of *McCall's* described the ritual that followed: "She sits down in front of a tea tray, delves into her large pocketbook for a match, lights the burner under the shallow hot-water kettle, and, rat-a-tat, launches the conversation. One minute, she is praising a book of memoirs she had read the previous night. The next minute she tells a guest that the pattern on her print dress looks like 'uncomfortable vegetables.' Asked for her opinion of women's liberation, she responds with an expression of distaste and a three-word put-down: 'It's . . . so . . . female.' "

Between sips of Jackson's of Piccadilly tea and barbed remarks on all kinds of subjects, Alice might receive dozens of phone calls—from her friends or her dressmaker or journalists asking for interviews. As a finale to the afternoon's entertainment, she might treat her guests to her imitation of Eleanor, endeavoring somehow to get her teeth to protrude while she raised her low, well-modulated voice a few decibels in mimicry of her cousin's tremulous soprano.

After the last guest departed, she would dine at home alone with Joanna or go out to a dinner party. Even in her eighties, she attended as many as three or four dinner parties a week. Yet, no matter how late she got home, she would spend the remaining hours reading until dawn. A voracious reader, she favored poetry and nonfiction. At eighty-six, she still memorized verses that pleased her and could recite her favorite poems by heart. The poem she liked best described her own character, she said, with "humiliating accuracy." It was about a little green lizard who lived on King Solomon's wall and ended with the quatrain: "Yet when the little lizard was led to speak/Of the king when the king was dead/He had only kept track of the flies on the wall/For he was but a lizard after all."

At two-thirty in the afternoon, after sleeping since dawn, she got up, had a light meal, and then in her chaffeur-driven car, set out on a few errands. Until 1970 her car was an ancient Cadillac piloted by an elderly black chauffeur named Turner. He and Mrs. Longworth fought almost constantly about driving directions, but stayed together a long, long while, helped perhaps by a mutual interest in boxing. They even went to prizefights together.

Alice liked to tell the story of Turner's being sideswiped by a white man driving a car with South Carolina license plates. "Watch where you're going, you black bastard," the man yelled, whereupon Mrs. Longworth stuck her head out the window and yelled back, "Shut up, you white son of a bitch!"

Toward the end of her life, she suffered from emphysema, migraine headaches and glaucoma, but complained about these afflictions to no one. When she was seventy-two, one breast was removed because of cancer; the other was removed when she was eighty-six She joked about it: "I'm the only topless octogenarian at Georgetown University Hotel."

On her ninetieth birthday, in 1974, she spoke candidly about sex in the old days with *Washington Post* reporter Sally Quinn: "Homosexuality and lesbianism were fashionable in those days," she said, and then related a story about how another woman was in love with her when she lived in the White House. "Still, usually I thought it better to keep away from joking about the lesbian thing since my father was president. But you know, in those days, people were always having love affairs with their poodles and putting tiny flowers in strange places . . ."

As she grew very old, she herself became the target for "that malevolent detachment" which kept her from becoming truly intimate with others or committing herself deeply to anything. She called herself "a shriveled Twiggy," "an old crone," or "a loathsome combination of Phyllis Diller and Marie Dressler."

With old age, her malice toward others also softened a bit. Reappraising her feelings for Eleanor Roosevelt, she said: "As far as I'm concerned, Eleanor really came into her own after Franklin died. Before, she was too noble—a person who had gone down in one coal mine too many."

What she still hated, she admitted tartly, was going to parties with someone her own age. But by the time she died of cardiac arrest on February 20, 1980, at the age of ninety-six, she had no more contemporaries. "I'm an old fossil, a cheerful fossil," she said. Indeed, Teddy, Nick, Bye, Paulina, Franklin, Eleanor and a succession of Presidents were long gone, and she who had watched them come and go and commented on their behavior pitilessly had somehow survived for almost a century.

Spirited to the end, she was unafraid of death. She said that she regarded it as just another special occasion.

11

Groucho

"Marriage is the chief cause of divorce."

OFFSTAGE a professional comedian may turn out to be depressingly unfunny. Onstage he may depend on a stable of gag writers to keep him supplied with jokes. As a ventriloquist gives life to a dummy, so a staff of paid scribes creates his comic persona.

There was one professional comedian, however, whose adlib remarks and outrageous behavior were as funny as any material his writers created. This was Groucho Marx, who was so adept—and fecund—an improviser that when he appeared in a musical or on television, his writers and fellow actors were often as convulsed as his audiences.

A short man of spare build with unruly dark hair, Groucho always looked and acted like an unflappable con man. With a twitch of his thick black eyebrows or a deadpan shrug of his shoulders, he could instantly cut down the rich, the pretentious and the foolish. Ruthlessly, he mocked national institutions and political leaders, movie stars and ordinary people, and assailed with machine gun-like delivery in his down-to-earth New Yorkese the pompous clichés of his time. He was particularly adept at portraying a crook who could wiggle out of almost any situation, recognizing a fellow fleecer when he saw one. Once against his will his wife dragged him to a séance. When the medium, who called herself the Great Narobi, fell into a trance and asked the assembled group to start asking questions, Groucho raised his hand and inquired, "Narobi—what's the capital of North Dakota?"

He sought membership in a Hollywood beach club, but was told that Jews were unwelcome. "Since my children are only half-Jewish," he asked the membership committee, "can they go into the water up to their knees?"

The child of an immigrant couple, Groucho was never dazzled by glamour and position. At a White House garden party during the 40s, he listened to a band struggling through some marches and then said to his hostess, Eleanor Roosevelt, "Now I know why you travel so much."

At the same party another guest came up to Groucho and asked him if he knew where Mrs. Roosevelt was, as he wanted to talk with her. "She's upstairs filing down her teeth," Groucho replied.

Once he was a member of the audience watching the renowned magician Houdini perform what was known as his needle-threading act. In this display Houdini would put a handful of needles and a spool of thread into his mouth. When he opened his mouth again, all the needles would come out, threaded. Before starting the act, Houdini called for some member of the audience to come on stage and look into his mouth so as to make sure it didn't contain any needles already threaded. Groucho volunteered and climbed up on stage.

"Now, if you please, sir, look in my mouth and see if you

see anything in it," Houdini said to him, opening his mouth as wide as possible.

"Oh, I do see something," he cried.

"You do?" Houdini stared at him. "Well then, sir, tell the audience what you see."

"Pyorrhea," Groucho answered, and returned to his seat.

Even the aloof and mysterious Greta Garbo did not escape Groucho's impertinence. At the height of her career, he was riding in an elevator at MGM when she happened to step in. Garbo was wearing an enormous hat, slacks, and a mannish coat. As she stood in front of Groucho, he could not resist lifting the back of her hat, a motion which resulted in the front of the hat slipping down over her face. Miss Garbo was furious. "How dare you?" she said icily, pushing her hat up, and whirling around to confront the crude boor who had dared to touch her.

"Oh, I beg your pardon," Groucho replied. "I thought you were a fellow I knew from Kansas City."

Hollywood columnist Louella Parsons was also subjected to the Groucho treatment. One day she saw him without make-up at the Brown Derby and rushed over.

"Are you Harpo Marx?" she demanded.

"No," retorted Groucho. "Are you?"

Groucho went to visit a friend recovering from minor surgery in the hospital. As he got into the elevator, he told the operator, "Men's tonsils, please."

One night he was asked to attend a private screening of *Samson and Delilah*, starring Victor Mature and Hedy Lamarr. At the end of the screening, the producer of the picture asked Groucho what he thought of it.

"Well, I did have one major criticism," Groucho snapped.

"Criticism? And what was that?" the producer asked huffily.

"Well, how can you expect an audience to be excited by a

film where the leading man's bust is larger than the leading lady's?"

Once Groucho was talking to the Los Angeles director of civil defense. When Groucho asked him to describe his job, the director said that his main duty was to make every person in Los Angeles conscious of civil defense.

"That's a tremendous undertaking," replied Groucho. "It's hard enough just to see to it that everyone in Los Angeles is conscious."

Some of his best ad-libs were made offstage, where his only audience was a waiter or maître d'. He was once refused admission to a fancy Hollywood restaurant because he wasn't wearing a necktie. The maître d' said he was sorry.

"Don't be sorry," the comedian replied. "I can remember when I had no pants."

Peering over the maître d's shoulder, he spied a bald-headed man having dinner in the restaurant. "This makes no sense at all!" he shouted. "I can't have dinner in this joint because I'm not wearing a necktie, but that guy's also breaking the rules. He's having dinner without his hair."

Groucho's facile tongue probably caused him the most trouble when he and his first wife Ruth and their two children were going through customs after a trip to Europe. Groucho made even more of a stir in customs than Oscar Wilde, who during a trip to America had told a customs official that he "had nothing to declare except his genius." Groucho had bought an expensive watch and lighter combination at Dunhill's in London that he didn't want to declare. Ruth suggested that he slip the customs man a few dollars to keep him from going through their luggage too carefully. "Bribery is dishonest," Groucho replied. "I'll have nothing to do with it." But when it came time to fill out the Declaration of Purchases form he filled it out as follows:

Name: Julius H. Marx
Address: 21 Lincoln Road, Great Neck, Long Island
Born: Yes
Hair: Not Much
Occupation: Smuggler
Purchases: Wouldn't You Like to Know?

With this in hand, he turned to Ruth at the customs counter and whispered loudly, "Where is the opium? Is it still in your girdle?" Instantly, the family was escorted to the customs office, where they were stripped and searched for illicit drugs.

Groucho was never at a loss for a shattering retort. Who but Groucho, for example, would resign from a club he regretted having joined by sending the club's president this telegram: "I don't want to belong to any club that will accept me as a member." He was also adept at feigning an air of injured dignity. "Gentlemen," he once wrote to a magazine which had been publishing scurrilous articles about him, "If you continue to write nasty pieces about me, I shall be obliged to cancel my subscription."

Julius Henry Marx (alias Groucho) was born in New York City on or around October 2, 1890. The date is uncertain, since Groucho liked to shift around the facts of his early life more or less to suit himself. His father was Samuel Marx, sometimes known as "Frenchy," an Alsatian Jew who had migrated to the United States, and his mother was Minnie Schoenberg, a blonde Jewess from a small town in Germany. Before she met Frenchy on the Staten Island Ferry, Minnie had worked as a seamstress in a straw hat factory on New York's Upper East Side.

Groucho was named for his Uncle Julius, whom his mother mistakenly presumed to be a man of wealth. She reasoned that

Uncle Julius would be so flattered at having a child named for him that he would leave the family his money. As it turned out, Uncle Julius was a pauper and in fact owed Frenchy thirty-four dollars. When he died, he did indeed leave his entire estate to his namesake. According to Groucho, this estate consisted of a nine-ball Uncle Julius had stolen from a poolroom, a box of liver pills, and a celluloid dickey.

Groucho was the third of five boys. The other Marx brothers were Leonard (Chico), the eldest; Adolph (Harpo), Milton (Gummo), and Herbert (Zeppo). A first son, Manfred, had died shortly after birth, and Leonard—who was very like his mother in looks and personality—became her favorite child. The family lived in Yorkville, and Frenchy often had trouble paying the rent. He was a tailor by profession but an inept one, according to reports. "Our neighborhood was full of Pop's customers," Groucho later said. "They were easily recognizable in the street, for they all walked around with one trouser leg shorter than the other, one sleeve longer than the other, or coat collars undecided where to rest."

Minnie had an older brother, Al Shean, of the well-known vaudeville team of Gallagher and Shean. Al was highly successful, and watching him toss nickels to her boys and to the neighborhood children inspired Minnie to put her own sons in show business. "Where else but in the theater can people who don't know anything make such a grand living?" she said.

At the age of ten Groucho was singing soprano in the Gus Edwards vaudeville troupe. At fourteen he dropped out of school and never went back. Although he dreamed of becoming a doctor, when he saw an ad for a boy singer in vaudeville, he trudged up five flights of stairs to the top floor of a dingy tenement, where a middle-aged man wearing lipstick and a blue kimono sat interviewing applicants for the job. The man's name was Robin Larong. After escorting Groucho up to the tin roof of the tenement, where thirty other boys his age were practicing their tap dancing, Larong asked Groucho to sing. Groucho obliged by belting out the popular tune, "Love Me and the World is Mine" with such verve and gusto that he was immediately hired as a member of the Larong Trio. He was understandably thrilled.

Several weeks later when the trio was playing in Cripple Creek, Colorado, Larong secretly left town after the trio's performance. He was never seen or heard from again. The third member of the trio also vanished, taking with him Groucho's two weeks' salary (eight dollars in all) which Groucho had kept hidden under his mattress and a pair of socks. Stranded and broke, Groucho applied for a job driving a grocery wagon between Cripple Creek and Victor, Colorado. Although the only horses he had ever driven were those on the merry-go-round at Coney Island, he told the grocery store owner he had been brought up on a ranch in Montana. His first trip from Cripple Creek to Victor proved to be his last. After a hair-raising ride over a curving mountain road, with a sheer drop of four thousand feet on one side, Groucho, clinging to the reins, careened into Victor's main street. There, one of the horses whinnied and dropped dead. Overcome with horror, Groucho ran all the way back to Cripple Creek, where he hid out in a boardinghouse until his mother sent him train fare to New York.

After a dismal stint cleaning wigs for a theatrical wigmaker, he was only too happy to join the act that Minnie had put together for her sons. It was called the Three Nightingales, a perfect name, Minnie thought, because, as she told Groucho, "everyone knows nightingales spend all their time singing." In the beginning, the act featured Gummo, Groucho, and a female singer. According to Groucho, the girl was the only member of the group who knew how to sing and not too well at that because she was always wandering off-key. "The other two Nightingales' voices were in the process of changing and from day to day no one could tell what sounds would emerge from their gifted throats," he said.

Minnie attired the trio in yachtsmen's clothes—white suits, straw hats and white shoes. Groucho asked his mother why she had picked these outfits, and she told him that Bloomingdale's had been selling white duck suits that morning for $9.98 and since summer was over, straw hats and white shoes were also going cheap.

A few months later, Minnie went back to Bloomingdale's for two more white suits. Harpo had joined the group as a bass singer although he had no vocal talent whatever, and the girl singer had been replaced by a boy tenor with perfect pitch. The name of the act was now the Four Nightingales, and in time it would be made up solely of the Marx brothers—Chico, Harpo, Zeppo and Groucho.

As the boys' voices continued to change, they realized that the only way to keep the act together was to make it a comedy act. Wearing one of Minnie's old blonde wigs and carrying a basket of fake frankfurters, Groucho pretended to be a German comedian. His emergence as a full-fledged comic, however, took place in an open-air theater in Nacogdoches, Texas, where a runaway mule distracted the audience from the performance of the Four Nightingales. When the audience was at last persuaded to return to their seats, Groucho, instead of starting their act, said, "Nacogdoches is full of roaches," and then the brothers began a parody of their own act in a mocking, slapstick style that was to become distinctively their own.

It made a hit and other parodies followed, particularly one called "Fun in Hi Skule." For the next few years the four brothers appeared in a succession of ten-cent vaudeville theaters across the United States. They slept in cheap boardinghouses and third-rate hotels and somehow managed to survive the unscrupulous practices of tight-fisted stage managers and miserly landladies. One Christmas, they stayed at a boardinghouse in Elizabeth, New Jersey, which seemed a cut above the others since the tablecloths were changed twice a week. Unfortunately, with such stylish accommodations, the caste system prevailed, and the Marx brothers, being actors and hence considered déclassé, were not allowed to sit with the other guests in the dining room. They were relegated to a small separate table in a far corner.

On Christmas Day, all the guests gathered in the dining room. A turkey was ceremoniously brought in and served to all the permanent boarders, and then returned to the kitchen. The Marx brothers were ignored. Recalled Groucho, "Our plates were still as bare as the president of a nudist colony."

Soon a large covered casserole was brought in from the kitchen. Lifting the lid, the boys were shocked to see a large, gray mackerel which had been provided for their Christmas meal. Outraged, they marched out of the dining room without touching a morsel and went to the theater, where they performed an impromptu act about a dead mackerel. Still ravenously hungry when they returned to the boardinghouse, they sneaked down to the kitchen, raided the icebox, and discovering the remains of the turkey, ate every last bit of it. Then, finding the mackerel, which still had not been touched, they transferred it to the empty turkey platter and jammed a note into its gaping mouth. "The Black Hand," it said.

By morning they had left the premises forever.

In Williamstown, Massachusetts, a college town, the brothers were once on a bill with two beautiful sisters who were as shapely as they were untalented. Although the brothers had top billing, the audience, composed mostly of college boys, was obviously much more taken with the two voluptuous sisters. One evening, after the sisters had left the theater, Groucho was walking by their dressing room and noticed some shapeless garments dangling on a hook, which as Groucho said, "looked suspiciously like symmetricals," leg and thigh padding over which thin, underendowed women wore opera-length stockings. According to Groucho, "though you might look like an underfed turkey in the shower, once you donned these pads all your basic imperfections disappeared and your shape rose and fell in all the places where your Creator had originally played you a dirty trick."

Seized by an impulse he could not resist, Groucho grabbed the "symmetricals" and hid them in a dresser drawer in his hotel room. That night, when he went to the theater to get ready for his act, he confronted a scene of chaos. The girls were screaming that their padding had been stolen and they refused to appear without it. Since the only other competition was a dog act, the brothers' performance was a huge success. But Groucho's conscience bothered him. That night he couldn't sleep, and his mind kept dwelling on "those two poor, helpless, shapeless girls, with a substantial part of them reposing in my bureau drawer." The next morning, he slipped the "symmetricals" into a suitcase and went to the theater. After making sure no one was looking, he hung the padding back on its hook.

"The girls appeared that evening," he recalled. "They were a huge success, and, as usual, we flopped. But despite our inability to entertain the audience, I slept much better that night."

About this time the Marx brothers received the nicknames by which they would be known from then on. "Sherlocko the Monk" was a widely read comic strip of the day, and many vaudevillians imitated its style by choosing stage names like

Knockos, Bangos, Henpeckos and Tightwados. During a poker game backstage in Galesburg, Illinois, Art Fisher, a monologuist, named the brothers as he dealt them their cards. Adolph, who by then had changed his name to Arthur, became Harpo because he knew how to play the harp. Milton became Gummo because he always wore gumshoes or rubbers to keep from catching cold. Zeppo's nickname was inspired by a talented chimpanzee named Zippo who was the star of a popular act. Fisher renamed Leonard Chico because his major interest in life was pursuing "the chickens" (girls). Because he looked dour and was a worrier, Julius Henry became Groucho. He did not like his name. "I hate it," he confided many years later to Hector Arce, one of his biographers. "It's terrible. It sounds like I'm the kind of guy who goes around whipping little children."

In 1919, the Marx brothers had their first big success in a musical short called *Home Again*. They tried out the act at the Hippodrome in Chicago, and as a result of a glowing review from Percy Hammond in the *Chicago Tribune*, were booked at the opulent Palace Theater in New York, then considered the best of the big-time vaudeville theaters. The brothers were a big hit and played the Keith-Albee circuit for over a year. Appearing with them in the show was a blonde, blue-eyed dancer of Swedish descent named Ruth Johnson. She and Groucho fell in love and were married. Soon Ruth became pregnant, and a son, Arthur, was born. One night Groucho went to the hospital to see his wife and child. Absorbed in playing with his baby son, he totally forgot about his duties at the theater and when he remembered, arrived too late to paste on the crepe hair mustache he wore on stage. Quickly, he slapped some black greasepaint on his upper lip. The audience accepted the change, and the greasepaint mustache became one of his trademarks, together with his wiggly eyebrows and constant cigar. He had begun smoking in his late teens so that he would look older and more sophisticated. "My mustache is genuine," he maintained, however. "It belongs to my maid."

The brothers took *Home Again* to London, where it was acclaimed by audiences which had previously been bored by them. But E. F. Albee, the head of the Keith-Albee circuit, resented the fact that they had accepted employment without his approval. He banished them from his circuit and soon they were unable to find work even in small towns.

Although the Marx brothers did not know it, Albee's vindictive behavior was the making of their careers. Vaudeville was about to die, and movies were taking over. During a card game, Chico was approached by a man who said he was the largest pretzel manufacturer in Hackensack, New Jersey, but desired to become a Broadway producer, since his mistress longed to star in a musical. He yearned to fulfill her dream, he told Chico, but he was prepared to put up only twenty-five thousand dollars.

The show, which miraculously was produced for that amount, was called *I'll Say She Is*! Although nobody knew what the title meant, it was a rousing success, launching the brothers on Broadway and making their mother, the indomitable Minnie, deliriously happy. Just before opening night while she was standing on a chair being fitted for the evening gown she planned to wear to the premiere, she slipped and broke her leg. Refusing to miss the occasion, she donned her usual blonde wig and, gorgeously arrayed, was carried into the theater on a stretcher.

I'll Say She Is! ran for three years on Broadway and changed the brothers' lives. Harpo, in particular, became the darling of the Algonquin crowd, thanks to Alexander Woollcott, who considered him "a great clown." Groucho, however, did not care for the Algonquin set or their conversation. "The admission fee was a viper's tongue and a half-concealed stiletto. It was a sort of an intellectual slaughterhouse . . . ," he said. He found Woollcott especially offensive and said he felt sick to his stomach when he heard Woollcott humiliating a slow waiter by ordering "muffins filled with pus."

Groucho felt more at home at the Hillcrest Country Club in Los Angeles. After he moved to California, he and some fellow comedians had lunch there so often they decided to form a Round Table of their own. Members of this West Coast Round Table included George Jessel, Eddie Cantor, Milton Berle, George Burns, Danny Thomas, Danny Kaye and the Marx brothers, except for Chico, who preferred his daily pinochle game at the Friars Club. Unlike the Algonquin Round Table, which had a membership that was constantly changing, the Hillcrest Round Table had a fixed number of members and admitted only men. Most of the jokes exchanged there were unprintable.

Like his brothers, Harpo found the rowdy Hillcrest group more congenial than the group at the Algonquin. "There was little conversation as such," he recalled. "It was a wide open competition to see who could get the most laughs, a running game of 'Can You Top This?' It was never dull. We had among us three of the funniest men of our time, George Burns, George Jessel and Groucho Marx, and it was among us, where no holds were barred, that they were at their funniest.

"When Jessel launched into one of his monologues, even his friend Julius kept quiet. Otherwise, Groucho was the Round Table's heckler-at-large. He 'left-jabbed' us to death in his sneaky, soft voice, with his cracks and asides. No punch line was safe from Groucho's counterpunch. No man, at the Round Table, or elsewhere, ever dared to slug it out with Groucho."

Like many another natural-born wit, Groucho never cared to probe deeply into the roots of his genius. Humor, he believed, should not be subjected to minute scrutiny. "As a lad, I don't remember knocking anyone over with my wit. I'm a pretty wary fellow, and I have neither the desire nor the equipment to analyze what makes one man funny to another man. I have read many books by alleged experts, explaining the basis of humor and attempting to describe what is funny and what isn't. I doubt if any comedian can honestly say why he is funny and why his next-door neighbor is not."

Groucho actually longed to be a writer. His best friends, the men he most admired—George S. Kaufman, S. J. Perelman, Norman Krasna—were all professional writers. Writers, he felt, were the real creative force in show business, and actors were merely mouthpieces for their talent. Groucho read avidly and feverishly and after overcoming his inferiority feelings about not having gone to college, he wrote a few articles which were printed in various magazines. H. L. Mencken reprinted an article Groucho wrote for Franklin P. Adams in the *New York World*. "Nothing I ever did as an actor thrilled me more," Groucho said.

As the years passed, he tried to broaden his literary horizons with a play, *Time for Elizabeth* (1948), which he wrote with Norman Krasna. He also wrote an autobiography, *Groucho and Me* (1959); unlike many books supposedly written by the great, it was not ghostwritten but composed entirely by himself. His correspondence was voluminous and highly literary. His letters to well-known people, including T. S. Eliot, James Thurber, Fred Allen and Harry S. Truman, were published by Simon & Schuster in 1967 under the title *The Groucho Letters*.

The letter was one of Groucho's favorite mediums for expressing his wit, although he also enjoyed injecting a touch of wry humor into the usually humorless chore of writing dust-jacket blurbs for friends' books. He wrote a blurb for Perelman's anthology, *Dawn Ginsberg's Revenge*, which read: "From the moment I picked up your book until I laid it down, I was convulsed with laughter. Some day I intend reading it."

Groucho's letters were filled with his opinions on many subjects. "I have no advice to give to young actors," he wrote. "To young, struggling actresses, my advice is to keep struggling. If you struggle long enough, you will never get into trouble and if you never get into trouble, you will never be much of an actress." On the institution of marriage, he wrote: "As for marriage, I know hundreds of husbands who would gladly go home if there weren't any wives waiting for them. Take the wives out of marriage and there wouldn't be any divorces. But then, someone might ask, what about the next generation? Look, I've seen some of the next generation—perhaps it's just as well if the whole thing ends right here."

To Eddie Cantor, who was writing a column for the Diner's Club magazine and wanted to know the two lines that had brought Groucho the biggest laughs in his career, he wrote: "The two biggest laughs that I can recall (other than my three marriages) were in a vaudeville act called *Home Again*. . . . One was when Zeppo came out from the wings and announced, 'Dad, the garbage man is here.' I replied, 'Tell him we don't want any' . . . The other was when Chico shook hands with me and said, 'I would like to say good-bye to your wife,' and I said, 'Who wouldn't?' "

To Bernice Connor, senior editor of *McCall's*, who had asked him to list the items he kept in his glove compartment in connection with an article on cars the magazine was planning to publish, he replied:

April 15, 1963

Dear Miss Connor:

You ask what I keep in my glove compartment. The last time I looked I had a woman's bikini, one half a cheese sandwich without mustard and a letter from the finance company saying that if I don't pay the $5,000 I owe on the $5,000 car, they will take the matter into their own hands. If they do, they'll find it pretty messy in that glove compartment.

Any further information you may want will have to come from my attorney, Schrecklichtheit, Schrecklichtheit and Meyer.

Sincerely yours,

Groucho Marx

In 1925, Groucho appeared with his brothers in *The Cocoanuts*, a satire on the Florida land boom written for them by George S. Kaufman, Morrie Ryskind and Irving Berlin. Knowing the brothers' reputation for zany ad-lib behavior on stage, Kaufman had to be talked into writing the script by the play's producer, Sam Harris. "I'd rather write for the Barbary apes," Kaufman reportedly said, but later he relented enough to let Groucho tamper with some of his lines, the only actor ever permitted to do so.

Playing the part of a society dowager in *The Cocoanuts* was an imperious thirty-four-year-old widow named Margaret Dumont, who was soon to become a vital part of the Marx brothers' entourage. Because of Groucho's constant ad-libbing, the show was never the same, and the audience was treated to a new version every night. Some people saw *The Cocoanuts* as many as twelve times. Even staid Calvin Coolidge attended a performance. When Groucho heard he was in the audience, he stepped to the footlights and ad-libbed, "Aren't you up past your bedtime, Calvin?" At another performance, he reportedly interrupted a scene and stepped to the footlights. "Is there a doctor in the house?" he asked. When a doctor stood up, Groucho said, "If you're a doctor why aren't you at the hospital making your patients miserable instead of wasting time with that blonde?"

With the advent of sound, the madcap Marx brothers seemed naturals for talking pictures. In 1929, the brothers filmed *The Cocoanuts* and in the next year, *Animal Crackers*. Both pictures were made in Paramount's Long Island studio because Chico, Harpo and Groucho were still appearing in *Animal Crackers* on Broadway.

In 1929, Minnie died of a cerebral hemorrhage after spending the evening at Zeppo's. She was sixty-five years old. Several weeks later, on October 24, the stock market crashed, and within two days Groucho had lost his life's savings of $240,000. Fearful of becoming a pauper, he began to suffer from insomnia. It was to plague him for the rest of his life and become a source of intense annoyance to his friends. When he was unable to sleep, he would call someone up in the middle of the night and insult him.

"This is Professor Waldemar Strumbelknauff. Aren't you ashamed of yourself, beating your children that way? If you were a man you'd come over here and knock my teeth out. If you were half a man, you'd knock half my teeth out . . . This is Groucho. How are you? As if I really care." And then he'd slam down the receiver.

In 1931, tired of Broadway, Groucho moved out to Hollywood, where he and his brothers made several more films. These included *Monkey Business* (1931), *Horse Feathers* (1932), *Duck Soup* (1933) and the highly popular *A Night at the Opera* (1935) which was followed by a sequel, *A Day at the Races* (1937). Of the fourteen pictures he made, Groucho always said he liked these last two the best. They were both produced by Irving Thalberg, MGM's wonder boy.

Groucho and Thalberg were scarcely kindred spirits. Groucho and his brothers created havoc wherever they went, while Thalberg, ever mindful of his top executive role, was polite but distant, and at times intensely irritating to actors. In fact, Thalberg often forgot that he had made an appointment with an actor or a writer and sometimes weeks or even months went by before the hapless visitor was finally admitted to his sanctum. Dorothy Parker and John Steinbeck were among the people who spent weeks "waiting for Thalberg." Steinbeck hung around Hollywood for six months before he found out why Thalberg had sent for him. George S. Kaufman, who was forced to cool his heels for days in Thalberg's outer office, announced to his fellow sufferers: "On a clear day you can see Thalberg."

Never ones to sit around when they could create a little mischief, the Marx brothers decided to take action when they were asked to wait in the usual fashion. Groucho and his siblings each lit two cigars and, lying down outside Thalberg's office, began smoking and puffing the smoke into the crack under the door. A few minutes later, Thalberg opened the door excitedly. "I smell smoke. Is there a fire?" he asked.

"Oh, no," they replied, smiling up at him from the floor. "There's the Marx brothers."

Thalberg, a thin, slightly built man who lived almost entirely for his work, had the disconcerting habit of conducting several story conferences at once in different offices. He would flit from one office to the other, offering suggestions and criticisms to the occupants, but never staying for more than a few minutes.

"We had just started discussing a comedy scene one afternoon in his office when he said, 'Hold it, boys, I'll be back in a minute,' " Groucho recalled. "The minute stretched to two hours. A few days later, he repeated the trick. The third time, we got angry. We rolled all the steel filing cabinets against the two doors and wouldn't allow him back in his office until he promised he wouldn't walk out on us again.

"Two days passed. We had just begun another conference when he again excused himself . . . In his absence we lit the logs in the fireplace and sent to the studio commissary for baking potatoes. When Thalberg returned, he found us all sitting naked in front of a roaring fire, busily roasting mickeys over the flames. He laughed and said, 'Wait a minute, boys!' He then phoned the commissary, and asked them to send up some butter for the potatoes. He never walked out on us again."

Groucho and his brothers loved elaborate practical jokes. Acting with the Marx brothers was a risky business at all times. Attractive young actresses were favorite scapegoats. Often, when a pretty girl went off-stage to change her costume, she would find wet paper in her slippers and the arm and leg holes of her costume sewn together.

Onstage, the jokes became even more diabolical. They were sometimes physically punishing, especially when the brothers assailed their feminine assistants with stage props or goosed them as they attempted an intricate dance routine. Maggie Irving, who appeared in *Animal Crackers*, recalled the show's final scene in which she played Madame DuBarry. Wearing a white wig and an enormous ruffled hoop over a satin and bejeweled leotard, she walked in regally and in a moment heard laughter from the audience. Unable to imagine what was causing it, she kept walking about the stage and as the laughter kept rising, finally sat down on a small chair and spread out her huge hoop. It was so voluminous that she hadn't realized somebody was under it.

It was Harpo.

Groucho walked over and asked her what she'd like to eat. Harpo's hand shot out from under the skirt, holding a telephone. Groucho took it and said, "Waiter, will you bring some ice water up to ten?"

But perhaps the most constant victim of their on stage bawdiness was Margaret Dumont, "Old Ironsides," as Groucho called her. She had acquired the nickname because she protected herself by wearing whalebone corsets after Groucho tripped her with a billiard cue once. This armor unfortunately did not offer much protection from all the punishment she had to undergo.

Early in her career Miss Dumont liked to wear dresses with long trains on stage. Groucho enjoyed following her, impishly leaping from one side of the train to the other as a boy might leap over a brook. One night he landed on the train. Miss Dumont continued her walk, and with a ripping sound, her whalebones were exposed to view.

Groucho said that Margaret Dumont never understood any of their jokes, and that once she asked him what the true meaning was of his line in *Duck Soup*, "Remember that we're fighting for this woman's honor, which is probably more than she ever did."

For the stately, dignified Miss Dumont, touring with the brothers must have been a nightmare. Harpo stole her wig, and once when she was sleeping soundly in her berth on a train, the railroad conductor, whose pants had been unceremoniously removed by the boys, was thrown in on top of her.

Miss Dumont did what any sane woman would do under the circumstances. She screamed.

One night, when they were on tour in Indianapolis, Miss Dumont, Maggie Irving and her mother ran into Groucho in the elevator of the hotel where they were staying. They rode up to the fifth floor together, and as they walked down the corridor, Groucho noticed the house detective watching some men playing cards. As the women went on to their rooms, he stopped to ask the detective what he was doing, and the detective replied that he was watching the men to make sure they didn't do anything illegal.

"As far as I can see, these men have committed no crime," Groucho said. "You're wasting your time, especially when you could be putting a stop to real evil. Did you see that woman—the very large woman who was walking with the two thinner women down the corridor only a few seconds ago? She's the most notorious hooker on the East Coast."

The detective's eyes blazed. "You don't say!" he exclaimed.

"There's practically no man from here to Florida who hasn't slept with her," Groucho told him. "Except for myself, of course. I find women of her type loathsome. In fact, if she's still here tomorrow, I'm leaving this hotel."

His curiosity piqued, the detective stopped watching the card players and started staking out Margaret Dumont.

The following evening, after she had returned to the hotel, Miss Dumont ran into the detective as he loitered just outside her door.

Politely she tried to engage him in conversation, but he did not respond. As she was putting her key into the lock, the door was pulled open by none other than Groucho in his greasepaint mustache and pajamas, a douche bag dangling from his wrist. "You made me wait!" he shouted at her. "I'll never forgive you!" He stormed past Miss Dumont and the detective and vanished. Flushed with embarrassment, Miss Dumont entered her room with the detective close behind her. There, lying on the bed, was Chico wearing only his underdrawers. Over his dark curly wig he sported a funny little hat. When he heard her come in, he put down the racing sheet he was reading and got up. "Oh, I see you're behind schedule," he said. "Well, make it quick with him because I'm coming back in half an hour." No sooner had he left the room than the closet door opened. Zeppo emerged, bare-chested, his middle draped with a hotel towel, his thighs wrapped in paper laundry bags. "It's not fair," he wailed. "I'm the youngest, and even though I've already paid you, you're always standing me up with another man."

Miss Dumont tried to explain about the Marx brothers and their fondness for practical jokes but could only manage to cry instead. The detective started questioning her, but no sooner had he opened his mouth than he heard the sound of running water in the bathroom and went to investigate. Seated in a bubble-filled tub was Harpo wearing a red wig and nothing else except for a jaunty bow tie around his neck. When the detective pulled him out of the tub, he discovered that Harpo was wearing an additional accessory—a necktie which boasted a Windsor knot tied around his penis.

Deciding that the joke had gone far enough, one of the guests, who had recognized the Marx brothers wandering around the hotel corridors in varying states of undress, told the detective their real identities and swore that Miss Dumont was not a hooker but the tormented victim of one of their outrageous pranks.

As for Miss Dumont, she packed her bags, checked out of the hotel, and tried to take the first train back to New York, but Groucho caught up with her at the station and talked her out of leaving. He explained that the prank was "all in good fun," and they would never subject her to such an ordeal again. Unfortunately she believed him.

No matter where they went, the Marx brothers seemed to have a tireless interest in removing their clothes. Once Groucho and Harpo were invited to a bachelor dinner at a fashionable New York steakhouse. Knowing that the restaurant had an automatic elevator which opened directly into the dining room of each floor, the brothers thought it would be funny to bring a suitcase along, get into the elevator and strip naked. When the elevator arrived at the dining room where they were expected, they would step out wearing only straw hats and carrying their valises.

"As the elevator doors slid open, the two practical jokers made their grand entrance," Groucho recalled. "But something had gone wrong. Instead of the hearty roar of masculine laughter that we anticipated, three women fainted and the rest of them started screaming for the police! It seems that friends of the bride were giving her a dinner that same evening on the floor above. In our eagerness and excitement, we had pressed the wrong button in the elevator!"

Panicking, the brothers ran back to the elevator, but the doors had already closed. They looked for the stairs, but they were not to be found. "Apparently some enemy of ours had removed them," Groucho said. Finally, they spotted a large rubber plant in the corner and hid behind it. A headwaiter eventually covered them with two tablecloths. After stammering their apologies to the horrified ladies, they were taken to the basement, where they sheepishly dressed.

Neither Harpo nor Groucho was invited to the wedding.

After Thalberg died, Groucho, who had never truly enjoyed movie-making, lost interest in films. "I continued to appear in them, but my heart was in the Highlands. The fun had gone out of picture-making. I was like an old pug, still going through the motions, but now doing it solely for the money," he said. One day, after being forced to hang upside down for hours on a ladder suspended from a prop plane on the set of *A Night in Casablanca* (1946), he realized he was too old for that sort of thing and decided to retire from the movies as soon as possible. The last picture he made with his brothers was *Love Happy* in 1949. In later years, he made solo appearances in such films as *Double Dynamite* (1951), *The Story of Mankind* (1957) and *Skidoo* (1968).

In 1947 Groucho appeared on radio with Bob Hope in a once-a-year special called "The Walgreen Show." In the middle of a skit Groucho threw away the script and began to ad-lib with Hope. Most of their remarks were dirty as well as funny, particularly several concerning a notorious Los Angeles madam, and ended up on the cutting room floor. Observing them both from backstage, however, was a producer, John Guedel, who had originated "People Are Funny," a show that was responsible for Art Linkletter's success on radio.

Impressed by Groucho's talent for off-the-cuff remarks, Guedel suggested that he do a new quiz show, in which the quiz would serve mostly as an excuse for Groucho to interview the contestants. He could extemporize as much as he pleased. The show premiered on ABC in 1947. It was called "You Bet Your Life" and was sponsored by the Elgin-American Compact Company, which soon ran out of compacts, so great was the demand from the delighted radio audience.

For the show Groucho replaced his greasepaint mustache with a real one and wore business clothes instead of his former black frock coat. The radio audience was tickled with his brash remarks and insults, which included the sentence, "No matter how badly I dress, I look as good as the audience." It was a rare contestant who failed to evoke some typical Groucho-ism. To a tree surgeon: "Tell me, Doctor, did you ever fall out of a patient?" To elderly newlyweds: "I'll never forget my wedding. They threw vitamin pills." To a test pilot: "I could never be a test pilot. I get dizzy licking an airmail stamp." To a middle-aged schoolteacher who came on the show and claimed she was approaching forty: "From which direction?" To a tongue-tied contestant: "Either this man is dead or my watch has stopped." To another contestant: "I never forget a face, but in your case, I'm going to make an exception." To a milkman and his girlfriend: "Well, you're a nice couple, and I hope the two of you have many half-pints."

With nonchalant daring, Groucho tackled topics that other radio comedians had shunned. He interviewed a Mrs. Story who had given birth to twenty-two children. "I love my husband," she enthused. "I like my cigar, too," Groucho replied, "but I take it out once in a while." This remark was deleted before it got on the air.

In record time Groucho deflated a minister who said to him, "Groucho, I want to thank you for all the enjoyment you've given the world." Without hesitation, Groucho retorted, "And I want to thank you for all the enjoyment you've taken out of it."

Not all of the humor on "You Bet Your Life" was spontaneous. Staff writers prepared many of the gags, as did Groucho himself after he was presented with a list of the contestants and their various occupations. The show was pre-recorded since the networks dared not chance a live show because of Groucho's tendency to slip in off-color remarks. It usually ran an hour and a half before being edited to 26 minutes. "Groucho didn't want to get that closely involved in the preparation," head writer Bernie Smith told Hector Arce. "He wanted to be fresh when he went out there. We had a pretty good idea, but time after time Groucho would come out there, and be wild, and we had no idea of what was happening. That's when we had the great shows. When he was at his peak you could never write for this man. He was much better than any writer could be."

In 1950, after running four years on radio, "You Bet Your Life" was bought for television by NBC. A rubber duck which descended on a string when the "secret word" was mentioned and other gimmicks brightened up the format. Week after week, it ran for eleven years, winning, among other prizes, an Emmy in 1951.

Because he invented so many funny lines and was the instigator of so many wild pranks, many people presumed that Groucho Marx's life was a constant round of fun. It is true that he reveled in his own power over an audience, but Groucho was a bedeviled man tormented by doubts about himself and others.

An intensely private person who was loath to reveal anything about himself, he often used his wit as a shield against a world he distrusted. "I am a serious man with a comic sense," he said. Perhaps afraid that if he acted normally he might be ultimately rejected, he took the offensive and lashed out at people with a barrage of insults and wisecracks. Although many of his friends were amused by his insolence, others found his compulsive one-liners wearing.

Even when he was wealthy and known all over the world, the very mention of a movie star who was unable to find work could upset him to the point where he could not sleep for days. "As I grew successful, the one thing that continually haunted me was the fear of being destitute in my old age," he wrote. "I realize that this is not an uncommon fear, but in my case the fright was imbedded so deep in my psyche that no day passed without my being chilled at the mere thought of it." In such a mood, he would subject his household to sudden economies, skimping on small purchases while continuing to splurge on luxuries. His wives were not allowed to buy anything without his say-so; his children were never given lessons in such things as piano or ballet because he felt they were an unnecessary expense. These quixotic beliefs caused considerable friction in all the households he headed.

More than any of his brothers, he valued marriage and serene domesticity, yet, ironically, his marriages were marred by strife, anguish and turmoil. He married three times. All his wives were considerably younger. All three were Gentiles. He married his first wife, Ruth Johnson, on February 4, 1920, in a ceremony that might have taken place in a vaudeville house. Piqued because several clergymen had refused to marry a Jew and a Gentile, he heckled the justice of the peace who finally performed the service. When the judge said "We are gathered here to join this couple in holy matrimony," the groom quipped, "It may be holy to you, Judge, but we have other ideas." Somewhat taken aback, the judge nevertheless managed to conduct the rest of the service, no doubt breathing a sigh of relief when he came to the point where he asked the husband-to-be, "Do you, Julius, take this woman to be your lawful wedded wife?"

"We've gone this far," retorted Groucho. "We might as well go through with it."

Though he uttered these bum jokes in jest, they seemed to symbolize his inherent suspicion and distrust of women and marriage. All his life Groucho preferred the company of men to women. Females, preferably non-Jewish females, were pretty adornments created to arouse one's lust or the envy of other men. "The trouble with marriage is you have to marry a woman—the last person in the world you could possibly have anything in common with," he complained. "The whole concept of marriage is wrong. It can never work except between two men, both of whom like baseball and have separate incomes."

Groucho was divorced from Ruth in 1942. Three years later he married Catherine (Kay) Gorcey, a model, by whom he had a daughter, Melinda. This marriage ended in divorce in 1950. In 1953, when he was past sixty, he married Eden Hartford, a twenty-four-year-old former model. They were divorced in 1969.

All of Groucho's wives were beautiful and inexperienced, and none of them had the intelligence and stamina to cope with such a moody, difficult man. At home, Groucho preferred to live in a world of his own, practicing his guitar for hours on end, reading till late into the night, or listening endlessly to his Gilbert and Sullivan records. He had an intense interest in W. S. Gilbert, the librettist of the Savoy operas, and identified with him. Both men were geniuses at wordplay, were crochety and argumentative, liked to make fun of older females, were fond of practical jokes and crazy about children and very young, very pretty girls. (At seventy-five, Gilbert died of a heart attack while trying to rescue a lovely nymphet he had invited to a lake for a swim.)

Groucho's eccentricities at first seemed amusing and rather lovable to his wives. But as time went on, his compulsive habits and routines became maddening. Even if dinner guests were only ten minutes late, Groucho would insist that the meal be served at the appointed hour and would sit down and start eating without them. At a party he would leave his guests at an early hour, telling them to "go ahead and get drunk on my booze and make fools of yourselves—I don't care because I'm going to bed."

He insisted on doing all the marketing for the household and after the children were born, spent all his free time at home with them, bathing and diapering them and supervising their play. He loved them when they were babies, but as they grew older, he seemed to lose interest, and quite often heckled them and insulted them, as though they were guests on his show. In every marriage he inevitably reached a point where he began baiting and sneering at his wife. Unable to endure the constant criticism, his wives, one by one, took to drink as an escape. By the time they found the courage to divorce him, all three had become alcoholics.

He had two children by his first marriage, Arthur and Miriam. In her maturity, Miriam succumbed to emotional illness and alcoholism, spending a good portion of her life in institutions. Arthur, his oldest child and only son, was able to establish his own identity only when he became a writer. He is the author of several books, including two about his father, *Life With Groucho* (1954) and *Son of Groucho* (1972), and was the co-author, with Robert Fisher, of a 1970 Broadway musical, *Minnie's Boys*, which depicted the Marx brothers' early years in show business. Although Arthur spent much of his life struggling to break free of his father, he could obviously not resist writing about him and in a spirit of forgiveness said, "A giant's shadow often falls a great distance."

Melinda, Groucho's daughter by Kay Gorcey, his second wife, was his favorite child, and when she was a little girl, he loved to show her off on his TV show, "You Bet Your Life," where she sang duets with him. Later their relationship became stormy, but they were reconciled just before he died.

Groucho's health gradually deteriorated as he grew older, and he suffered from a series of strokes which affected his mind. As in the case of W. S. Gilbert who became an affable man in his old age, the gentle, kindly side of Groucho's nature rose to the surface toward the end of his life. It was said that he became an affectionate, sweet-tempered old man.

In the last six years of his life, Groucho's constant companion and live-in manager was a young red-haired actress in her thirties named Erin Fleming. Although he was ill, deaf and feeble, she persuaded him to resume his career with a series of one-night concert appearances. Three years before his death, he appointed her his guardian and temporary conservator of his estate. Claiming that she used undue influence, his children took Erin to court and had her removed as conservator. After Groucho's death, more legal wrangles followed, involving, among other issues, Groucho's legacy to Erin of $150,000, plus control of his movie and television rights.

Julius Henry Marx died on August 19, 1977, in Cedars-Sinai Hospital in Los Angeles. He was eighty-six years old.

He left behind a person named Groucho, a special creation, with a gliding seductive walk, eyebrows like twin commas, and an outrageous greasepaint mustache—a kind of marvelous ventriloquist's dummy whom Julius Marx had taken nightly from its box and imbued with life. When Groucho opened his mouth, people laughed—and are still laughing.

Groucho lives!

Chief Sources

In researching this book, I have read hundreds of magazine and newspaper articles on each of my subjects, but have listed as major sources only those articles and books which contained important information about the people herein described. Innumerable other books containing less significant biographical data, magazine and newspaper articles, profiles, theatrical scrapbooks and reference books have also been consulted, as well as all the published works and letters of my subjects. In the case of Tallulah Bankhead, Dorothy Parker and Oscar Levant, I have added information culled from personal interviews.

Writing this book would have been a vastly more arduous project had it not been for the men and women who have written illuminating biographies on some of my subjects. Their work is an indispensable source of information and should be read by anyone interested in further exploring the lives of American wits during the period. In the case of Robert Benchley, there has never been any biography of him to compare with the affectionate book written by his son Nathaniel. As far as the Mizner brothers are concerned, the portraits of them both in *The Legendary Mizners*, written by the late Alva Johnston, are magnificent and reveal much previously unknown information about their lives and wit.

Alexander Woollcott:

Drennan, Robert, ed. *The Algonquin Wits*, Citadel Press, New York, 1968.

Ehrlich, Arnold W. "The Algonquin at 75," *New York Times Magazine*, October 16, 1977.

Gaines, James R. *Wit's End: Days and Nights of the Algonquin Round Table*, Harcourt Brace Jovanovich, New York, 1977.

Harriman, Margaret Case. *The Vicious Circle: The Story of the Algonquin Round Table*, Rinehart & Co., New York, 1951.

Harris, Jed. *A Dance on the High Wire*, Crown Publishers, New York, 1979.

Hoyt, Edwin P. *Alexander Woollcott, the Man Who Came To Dinner*, Abelard-Schuman, New York, 1968.

Marx, Harpo, with Rowland Barber: *Harpo Speaks!*, Bernard Geis Associates, New York, 1961.

Teichmann, Howard. *Smart Aleck. The Wit, World and Life of Alexander Woollcott*, William Morrow, New York, 1976.

Robert Benchley

Benchley, Nathaniel. *Robert Benchley*, McGraw-Hill Book Co., New York, 1955.

Mrs. Robert Benchley's personal scrapbook, Theater Collection of the Performing Arts Research Center, The New York Public Library at Lincoln Center.

Bryan, J., III. "Funny Man: A Study in Professional Frustration," *The Saturday Evening Post*, September 23, 1939, and October 7, 1939.

Gaines, James R. *Wit's End: Days and Nights of the Algonquin Round Table*, Harcourt Brace Jovanovich, New York, 1977.

Graham, Sheilah. *The Garden of Allah*, Crown Publishers, New York, 1970.

Rosmond, Babette. *Robert Benchley: His Life and Good Times*, Doubleday, Garden City, New York, 1970.

Wilson, Edmund. *The Twenties: from Notebooks and Diaries of the Period* (ed. Leon Edel), Farrar, Straus & Giroux, New York, 1975.

Yates, Norris W. *Robert Benchley*, Twayne Publishers, Boston, 1968.

George S. Kaufman

Goldstein, Malcolm. *George S. Kaufman: His Life, His Theatre*, Oxford University Press, New York, 1979.

Gordon, Max, with Lewis Funke. "George S. Kaufman. A Profile," *Variety*, June 8, 1964.

Harriman, Margaret Case. *The Vicious Circle: The Story of the Algonquin Round Table*, Rinehart & Co., New York, 1951.

Hart, Moss. *Act One*, Random House, New York, 1959.

Levant, Oscar. *The Memoirs of an Amnesiac*, G. P. Putnam's Sons, New York, 1965.

______. *The Unimportance of Being Oscar*, G. P. Putnam's Sons, New York, 1968.

Marx, Harpo, with Rowland Barber. *Harpo Speaks!*, Bernard Geis Associates, New York, 1961.

Meredith, Scott. *George S. Kaufman and His Friends*, Doubleday, Garden City, New York, 1974.

Teichmann, Howard. *George S. Kaufman: An Intimate Portrait*, Atheneum Publishers, New York, 1972.

Thurber, James. "The Man Who Was Comedy," *Theatre Arts*, August 1961.

Dorothy Parker

Drennan, Robert, ed. *The Algonquin Wits*, Citadel Press, New York, 1968.

Gaines, James R. *Wit's End: Days and Nights of the Algonquin Round Table*, Harcourt Brace Jovanovich, New York, 1977.

Graham, Sheilah. *The Garden of Allah*, Crown Publishers, New York, 1970.

Harriman, Margaret Case. *The Vicious Circle: The Story of the Algonquin Round Table*, Rinehart & Co., New York, 1951.

Hellman, Lillian. *An Unfinished Woman: A Memoir*, Little, Brown, Boston, 1969.

Keats, John. *You Might As Well Live: The Life and Times of Dorothy Parker*, Simon & Schuster, New York, 1970.

Levant, Oscar. *The Unimportance of Being Oscar*, G. P. Putnam's Sons, New York, 1968.

"Dorothy Parker," in *Writers at Work: The Paris Review Interviews*, The Viking Press, New York, 1959.

Rosmond, Babette. *Robert Benchley: His Life and Good Times*, Doubleday, Garden City, New York, 1970.

Teichmann, Howard. *George S. Kaufman: An Intimate Portrait*, Atheneum Publishers, New York, 1972.

Wilson, Edmund. *The Twenties: from Notebooks and Diaries*

of the Period (ed. Leon Edel), Farrar, Straus & Giroux, New York, 1975.

Oscar Levant

Cerf, Bennett. *At Random: The Reminiscences of Bennett Cerf* (ed. Phyllis Cerf Wagner and Albert Erskine), Random House, New York, 1977.

"In Search of Frenzy," *Time*, August 28, 1972.

Kolodin, Irving. "The Trouble with Oscar," *Saturday Review*, September 9, 1972.

Levant, Oscar. *A Smattering of Ignorance*, Garden City Publishing Co., Garden City, New York, 1942.

______. *The Memoirs of an Amnesiac*, G. P. Putnam's Sons, New York, 1965.

______. *The Unimportance of Being Oscar*, G. P. Putnam's Sons, New York, 1968.

Marx, Harpo, with Rowland Barber. *Harpo Speaks!*, Bernard Geis Associates, New York, 1961.

Obituary, *New York Times*, August 15, 1972.

Parker, Dorothy. "Oscar Levant," in *Double Exposure* by Roddy McDowell, Delacorte Press, New York, 1966.

Targ, William. *Indecent Pleasures*, Macmillan, New York, 1975.

Zolotow, Maurice. *No People Like Show People*, Random House, New York, 1951.

W. C. Fields

Ford, Corey. *The Time of Laughter*, Little, Brown, Boston, 1967.

Johnston, Alva. "Legitimate Nonchalance," *The New Yorker*, February 2, 9, 16, 1935.

______. "Who Knows What Is Funny?", *Saturday Evening Post*, August 6, 1938.

Markfield, Wallace. "The Dark Geography of W. C. Fields," *New York Times Magazine*, April 24, 1966.

Monti, Carlotta, with Cy Rice. *W. C. Fields and Me*, Prentice-Hall, Englewood Cliffs, New Jersey, 1971.

Obituary, *New York Times*, December 26, 1946.

Taylor, Robert Lewis. *W. C. Fields: His Follies and Fortunes*, Doubleday, New York, 1941.

West, Mae. *Goodness Had Nothing To Do With It*, Prentice-Hall, Englewood Cliffs, New Jersey, 1959.

Zierold, Norman J. *The Child Stars*, Coward-McCann, New York, 1965.

Texas Guinan

The American Heritage History of the 1920's and 30's. American Heritage Publishing Company, New York, 1970.

Vanity Fair: A Cavalcade of the 20's and 30's, Amory, Cleveland, and Frederic Bradlee, eds. The Viking Press, New York, 1960.

Miss Guinan's own scrapbook (presented by John Stein), Theater Collection of the Performing Arts Research Center, The New York Public Library at Lincoln Center.

Hoffman, Jerry. Interview, *Los Angeles Examiner*, September 17, 1933.

Interview, *Chicago Herald and Examiner*, February 27, 1933.

Interview, *Los Angeles Evening Herald*, August 21, 1933.

Interview, *New York City Mirror*, September 12, 1933.

Interview, *Los Angeles Times*, September 17, 1933.

Interview, *Los Angeles Evening Herald*, September 19, 1933.

Mavity, Nancy Barr. Interview with Texas Guinan, *Cleveland Tribune*, October 1, 1933.

"Mob at Burial Rips Roses Off Guinan Coffin," *New York Herald Tribune*, November 13, 1933.

Obituary, Larry Fay, *New York Herald Tribune*, January 3, 1933.

______. *New York Evening Journal*, January 4, 1933.

Stein, John J., and Grace Hayward. *Hello, Sucker!* (unpublished biography on the life of Texas Guinan), © Republic Studios, Inc., North Hollywood, California, 1941.

Stevenson, Elizabeth. *Babbits and Bohemians: The American 1920s*, Macmillan, New York, 1967.

Stoddard, Theodore. *Luck Your Silent Partner*, Horace Liveright, New York, 1929.

"Texas Guinan Coming Back in Death," *New York World Telegram*, November 6, 1933.

"Tex Guinan's Death Laid to Chicago Fair Scourge," *New York Daily News*, November 11, 1933.

"Texas Guinan's Funeral Here," *New York Sun*, November 6, 1933.

"Throngs at Bier Bid Tex Goodbye," *New York Sunday News*, November 12, 1933.

Walker, Stanley. *The Night Club Era*, Frederick A. Stokes Co., New York, 1933.

Wilson and Addison Mizner

Amory, Cleveland. "The Old Palm Beach," *Diner's Club Magazine*, July 1961.

Coughlin Gene. "Prince of Pixies: The Wit of Wilson Mizner," *American Weekly*, June 11, 1950.

Johnston, Alva. *The Legendary Mizners*, Farrar, Straus and Young, New York, 1953.

Loos, Anita. *Cast of Thousands*, Grosset & Dunlap, New York, 1977.

Mizner, Addison. *The Many Mizners*, Sears Publishing Co., New York, 1932.

Obituary, *New York Herald Tribune*, April 4, 1933.

Phillips, Sidney. "Wilson Mizner: The Sage of the Hollywood Brown Derby," *Diner's Club Magazine*, December 1963.

Sullivan, Edward Dean. *The Fabulous Wilson Mizner*, Henkle Company, New York, 1935.

Tully, Jim. "California Playboy," *Esquire*, July 1938.

Tallulah Bankhead

Bankhead, Tallulah. *Tallulah: My Autobiography*, Harper & Brothers, New York, 1952.

Brian, Denis. *Tallulah, Darling: A Biography of Tallulah Bankhead*, Macmillan, New York, 1980.

Gill, Brendan. *Tallulah*, Holt, Rinehart and Winston, New York, 1972.

Harriman, Margaret Case. *The Vicious Circle: The Story of the Algonquin Round Table*, Rinehart & Co., New York, 1951.

Israel, Lee. *Miss Tallulah Bankhead*, G. P. Putnam's Sons, New York, 1972.

"Just a Dame from New England: Bette Davis Celebrates Fifty Years in Films," *Time*, April 14, 1980.

Loos, Anita. *Cast of Thousands*, Grosset & Dunlap, New York, 1977.

Obituary, *New York Times*, December 13, 1968.

Seldes, Marian. *The Bright Lights: A Theatre Life*, Houghton Mifflin Company, Boston, 1978.

"Tallulah," *Newsweek*, December 23, 1968.

Tunney, Kieran. *Tallulah: Darling of the Gods*, E. P. Dutton, New York, 1973.

Zolotow, Maurice. *No People Like Show People*, Random House, New York, 1951.

Alice Roosevelt Longworth

Alsop, Joseph. "Washington's Other Monument," *Vogue*, February 1, 1966.

Berg, A. Scott. *Maxwell Perkins: Editor of Genius*, Thomas Congdon Books (E. P. Dutton), New York, 1978.

Brandon, Harry. "A Talk with an 83-Year-Old Enfant Terrible," *The New York Times Magazine*, August 6, 1967.

Brough, James. *Princess Alice: A Biography of Alice Roosevelt Longworth*, Little, Brown, Boston, 1975.

Lash, Joseph P. *Eleanor and Franklin*, W. W. Norton, New York, 1971.

Longworth, Alice Roosevelt. *Crowded Hours: Reminiscences of Alice Roosevelt Longworth*, Charles Scribner's Sons, New York, 1933.

MacPherson, Myra. "Alice Longworth at 85," *Washington Post*, February 12, 1969.

______."Alice Roosevelt Dies . . . Dominated Society Nearly a Century," *Washington Post*, February 21, 1980.

"Malicious Wit" *Time*, March 3, 1980.

Obituary, *The New York Times*, February 21, 1980.

"Princess Alice: The End of a Reign," *Newsweek*, March 3, 1980.

Quinn, Sally. "Alice Longworth at 90," *Washington Post*, February 12, 1974.

______. "The Canny Candor of Alice Roosevelt Longworth," *Washington Post*, February 21, 1980.

Safire, William. "Weaned on a Pickle," *New York Times*, February 25, 1980.

Sheehan, Susan. "Washington's Wittiest Woman," *McCall's*, January 1974.

Sorensen, Theodore. *Kennedy*, Harper & Row, New York, 1965.

Teichmann, Howard. *Alice: The Life and Times of Alice Roosevelt Longworth*, Prentice-Hall, Englewood Cliffs, New Jersey, 1979.

vanden Heuvel, Jean. "The Sharpest Wit in Washington," *The Saturday Evening Post*, December 1965.

Walton, William. "Presidents She Has Known," *Washington Post*, February 12, 1969.

Groucho Marx

Adamson, Joe. *Groucho, Harpo, Chico and Sometimes Zeppo: A History of the Marx Brothers and A Satire on the Rest of the World*, Simon & Schuster, New York, 1973.

Arce, Hector. *Groucho: The Authorized Biography*, G. P. Putnam's Sons, New York, 1979.

Marx, Arthur. *Life with Groucho: A Son's Eye-View*, Simon & Schuster, New York, 1954.

______. *Son of Groucho*, David McKay, New York, 1972.

Marx, Groucho: *Groucho and Me*, Bernard Geis Associates, New York, 1959.

______. *The Groucho Letters: Letters from and to Groucho Marx*, Simon & Schuster, New York, 1967.

Marx, Groucho, with Hector Arce. *The Secret Word Is Groucho*, G. P. Putnam's Sons, New York, 1976.

Marx, Harpo, with Rowland Barber. *Harpo Speaks!*, Bernard Geis Associates, New York, 1961.

Obituary, *New York Times*, August 20, 1977.

Additional Sources

Blair, Walter, and Hamlin Hill. *America's Humor: From Poor Richard to Doonesbury*, Oxford University Press, New York, 1978.

Goodman, Jack, and Albert Rice. *I Wish I'd Said That!*, Simon & Schuster, New York, 1935.

Henry, Lewis C. *Humorous Anecdotes About Famous People*, Halcyon House, Garden City, New York, 1948.

Herzberg, Max John. *Insults: A Practical Anthology of Scathing Remarks and Acid Portraits*, Greystone Press, New York, 1941.

Joe Miller's Jests or the Wits Vade-mecum, facsimile of first edition (1739), compiled by John Mottley, Dover Publications, New York, 1963.

Mahony, Patrick. *Barbed Wit and Malicious Humor*, Citadel Press, New York, 1956.

Pearson, Hesketh. *The Lives of the Wits*, Harper & Row, New York, 1962.

Rourke, Constance. *American Humor: A Study of the National Character*, Harcourt Brace, New York, 1931.

White, E. B., and Katharine S. White, eds. *A Subtreasury of American Humor*, Coward-McCann, New York, 1941.